Cover photographs:
Chris Foote Wood (front, day)
Dave Trotter (back, night)

TINDALE TOWERS

NEW ART DECO MANSION

by
Chris Foote Wood

How Mike Keen's dream home was planned, designed and built 2005-2007

NORTHERN WRITERS

First published January 2008
Northern Writers
"Wor Hoos"
28 Cockton Hill Road
Bishop Auckland
County Durham DL14 6AH
www.northernwriters.co.uk
www.writersinc.biz

British Library Cataloguing in Publication Data
A catalogue for this book is available from the British Library.

ISBN 978-0-9553869-3-0

Typeset in Meta 12pt/14pt
Typesetting and origination, printed and bound by Lintons Printers Ltd, Beechburn, Crook, Co Durham DL15 8RA
www.lintons-printers.co.uk

for Mike

Tindale Towers: the House (or rather Mansion) that Mike built.

Chris Foote Wood

Contents

Introduction

A few words from Mike...

Welcome to my lifestyle. I created this property for comfort and convenience, not for profit. I could have bought a holiday home anywhere, but I get to enjoy this place 365 days a year, and it is only half a mile or two minutes from work. I do hope you like it as much as me and enjoy this book.

Mike Keen - a happy man

Mike Keen
Tindale Towers
Darlington Road
Bishop Auckland
County Durham
DL14 9AP

....and Chris

Chris Foote Wood

Planning applications rarely excite, but this one certainly did excite me. As the members of Wear Valley Council's planning committee trawled through their routine and rather boring weekly list of plans submitted for their approval, few could have realised just what was involved with Mike Keen's application to build a "house and garage" at Tindale Crescent near Bishop Auckland. For a start, the garage was a triple-double one. And the house? Or should I say, THE House!

As soon as the site was cleared, and without asking Mike's permission or even telling him, I started to take progress photographs. This is what I used to do when I had a "proper job" as a civil engineer over thirty years ago, before I gave it up to be a freelance journalist and broadcaster. At first I took pictures of Tindale Towers from the ground up purely for my own pleasure and interest. It was obvious from day one that this was to be something unusual and extraordinary, especially for the County Durham market town of Bishop Auckland. *"An Art Deco house in Bishop? You must be joking! And what's Art Deco anyway?"* was a typical response.

Over the months the idea formed in my mind of recording the birth of this fantastic addition to the Auckland landscape in a book. But to do so, I needed Mike Keen's approval, and the support of the various firms working on the job. My guess is that it took at least 300 people to create TT, and this book is a tribute to their professional skills and expertise. Most of all, this book is a tribute to the vision and generosity of Mike himself.

Chris Foote Wood
"Wor Hoos"
Bishop Auckland
January 2008

Sun Room

Peter Davies

Chapter One

Iconic building

Driving north up the A1(M), you cross the Yorkshire/Durham border shortly after passing Scotch Corner, so called because it stands at the junction with the A66 which leads to Scotland and Gretna Green. Once past Scotch Corner, it was said, eloping couples were safe from the hot-foot pursuit of any vengeful father bent on saving his daughter from the shame and degradation of an unsuitable marriage or worse, seduction and abandonment.

Just north of Scotch Corner you turn off the motorway along the B6275 road, leading to the pretty village of Piercebridge which spans the River Tees between two of England's north-eastern counties. This is the route taken by newly-appointed Bishops of Durham, on their way to their consecration in Durham Cathedral, rightly designated a World Heritage site. Midway over the bridge, between Yorkshire and County Durham, the new Bishop is ceremonially handed the Falchion Sword, symbol of his temporal power.

For centuries, the Bishops of Durham ruled as Princes in their own right. They made their own laws and administered justice. Their role was to rule what was in effect a state within a state, the object being to provide a buffer zone to protect the rest of England from invasion by the Scots. To this day, the Church Commissioners still own a good deal of land in County Durham (the only English County to put its name second) and the Bishop still lives in Auckland Castle, the Bishop's Palace, if only during his term of office. Hence the name of the adjoining town "Bishop Auckland." The Bishops of Durham used to have ten palaces, but now have to make do with just the one. The name Auckland, by the way, is generally reckoned to be derived from "Oak Land" for fairly obvious reasons.

The Bishop's Palace, or Auckland Castle, whichever you care to call it, is a magnificent building in a magnificent setting. While it still thrills us today, it is of course of its time. Tindale Towers, no more than two miles away, was never going to be a palace, although it does qualify as a mansion ("a large, imposing house" – Webster's dictionary). Tindale Towers is a very fine family home, and it is certainly imposing. Built 2005/07, it is very much of its time, combining classic design with modern building techniques. As owner Mike Keen has it: *"Tindale Towers is New Art Deco."*

Taking the Bishop's path through Piercebridge, the road takes you through another fine Durham village, Staindrop, and on past Raby Castle which played a crucial role in the Wars of the Roses. Next you come to West Auckland, crossing the original line of the Stockton & Darlington Railway – the world's first passenger steam railway - and on to St Helen Auckland where the parents of former Prime Minister Sir Anthony Eden (a Bishop Auckland lad) are buried. Then it's on to Tindale Crescent, on the outskirts of Bishop Auckland, with Tindale Towers to be seen prominently on the right.

Tindale village, in reality a suburb of Bishop Auckland, has expanded far beyond its original crescent. This is still a fine Victorian curved terrace, built to house employees of the North Eastern Railway. Tindale and the market town of Bishop Auckland are closely associated with the S & D Railway. Designed and built by Geordie colliery engineer George Stephenson, the S&DR was created in 1825 to carry coals from the Phoenix Pit at Witton Park, just up the road, to the river Tees at Stockton for onward shipment to London by sea. The canny Quaker businessmen who backed the Stockton & Darlington Railway realised they could boost their profits by carrying passengers as well as coal, the "black gold." The rest, as they say, is history.

Mike's New Art Deco Mansion

PlanArch Design

The quicker and more conventional way to get to Tindale and Bishop is to continue up the A1(M) past Scotch Corner, ignoring the turn-off to Darlington and taking the A68 – "the scenic route to Scotland" - at junction 58, and then the A6072 fork to Bishop Auckland. By-passing Heighington and Shildon – another railway town – Tindale Towers is the first building you see as you approach Tindale Crescent. You certainly cannot miss Mike Keen's dream home. It hits you in the eye, but unlike the French phrase "trompe l'oeil" (a trick of the eye) this is the reality, not a visual deception.

Tindale Towers makes a statement, a bold statement. It tells you that here is a district that is not afraid to innovate, that combines the best of the old with the best of the new. Let other places disappear under a tide of bland, "safe" buildings where nothing is allowed to stand out. On the site of his old bungalow and land that housed an ugly and unsightly collection of scrap cars, Mike Keen has created a building that makes best use of the site and is an asset to the area.

Tindale Towers is an iconic building. It came about because Mike Keen had the vision and the means to turn that vision into reality. Many people helped along the way, notably PlanArch director John Lavender and Arran Construction boss David Lee, and of course the teams they led. The planners of Wear Valley District Council, and indeed the councillors themselves, must take credit for backing a proposal that they might well have opposed. Building an Art Deco mansion on the edge of a former railway and mining town was a controversial proposal. Planning officers do not always welcome the unusual, and local councillors - and especially their constituents - can always find reasons for opposing ground-breaking, ambitious schemes such as this.

Mike's idea for a striking and unusual house was readily embraced by the local council, planners and councillors alike. After that, all that had to be done was to get the thing built. That is the story of this book.

Clear view

The Pool

The Bar

Guest bedroom

Balcony

Balcony detail

Carpetted stairs   Pictures by Peter Davies

Chapter Two

New Art Deco

The name Art Deco comes from the 1925 Paris art exhibition, the Exposition Internationale des Arts Décoratifs et Industriels Modernes. Arts Décoratifs became Art Deco. With its bold and simple lines, geometric shapes and intense colours, the Art Deco style has never dated and still looks modern today.

Most noteable for its application to architecture and particularly to large iconic buildings, Art Deco has also influenced the design of cars, ocean liners, houses, shops, banks, hotels, restaurants, railway stations, cinemas, films and computer games, as well as furniture and pottery. Above all, Art Deco is the ultimate in style, cool, elegant and sophisticated while appealing to almost all tastes.

Rejecting the fussiness of Art Nouveau, Art Deco has many influences: Cubism and other early twentieth-century avant-garde painting styles; increasing mechanization; streamlining and aerodynamic shapes. The Bauhaus School of design with its severe lines was another influence. The discovery of King Tutankhamen's tomb in Egypt in 1922 made the styles of ancient Egypt fashionable, a fascination that continues to this day. As well as ancient Egypt, Art Deco takes images from ancient Greece and Rome, Africa, India, the Far East, the Aztecs and Mayans, combining them in a modern, steamlined style.

While its lines are clean and unfussy, Art Deco denotes opulence, which came as a welcome change after the privations of the first World War. The style reached a peak in the 1930s but faded out in the 1940s and 1950s, its association with luxury unwelcome in an age of austerity and rationing. Improving living standards brought a revival of Art Deco in the 1960s, and the style is now accepted as part of modern living, just as it was in the 1930s.

When you say "Art Deco", the first thing most people bring to mind are iconic American skyscrapers like the Chrysler Building (1930) and the Empire State Building (1931), much copied by filmmakers and comic-strip cartoonists. Brooklyn-born architect William van Alen (1882-1954) designed the Chrysler Building, generally regarded as New York's greatest example of Art Deco architecture. It was faced with stainless steel, to reflect Chrysler car design. New York's first Art Deco building was the Barclay-Vesey building in lower Manhattan (1923), designed by architect Ralph Thomas Walker (1889-1973).

Another American architect, Raymond Hood (1881-1934) designed some of the most distinctive buildings in New York: the American Radiator (now American-Standard) Building (1924), the Daily News Building (1930), Radio City Music Hall (1932) and the RCA Building (1933) at Rockefeller Center, and the McGraw-Hill Building (1934). Hood also designed the Tribune Tower, Chicago (1924) and the Masonic Temple, Scranton, Pennsylvania (1930). Dramatic and bold with their geometric designs, these city skyscrapers were seen as the buildings of the future.

In Europe, Paris-born Robert Mallet-Stevens (1886-1945) promoted Art Deco architecture with the Paris Fire Station (1936) and various houses and other buildings. An early proponent of what became Art Deco was Finnish architect Eliel Saarinen (1873-1950). He designed the Finnish pavilion at the 1900 World's Fair in Paris, the Pohjola Insurance Building in Helsinki (1906) and the Helsinki railway station (1904-1914). In 1923 Saarinen moved to the USA where he and his son both designed outstanding buildings. The Helsinki railway station is one of the first recognised Art Deco buildings, if not the first. Its four giant statues, each holding a globe of light, are quintessential Art Deco.

Art Deco influenced the design of the French ocean liners Ile de France (1926) and Normandie (1932). Scores of cinemas built from the 1930s to the 1960s give homage to Art Deco – luxury, style and comfort for the price of a cinema ticket. Recent films like "King Kong" and "Batman" feature Art Deco buildings, as do the computer games Sim City 4 and Grim Fandango. Batman creator Bob Kane drew the first comic strip of his super-hero in 1940, so both Batman and Art Deco have stood the test of time.

The Art Deco style is instantly recognisable, even by people who can't recall or don't even know its name. Yet no two Art Deco buildings are the same. Mike Keen's Tindale Towers mansion in North East England continues the tradition. It uses Art Deco as a basic design concept while including many other elements. This makes Mike's dream home a unique building, an unusual and dramatic addition to the County Durham market town of Bishop Auckland. Mike calls it "New Art Deco", and why not?

A fine house in Colwyn Road, Llandudno

Merlin House, Purley Way, Croydon

A few examples of Art Deco I spotted on my travels - Chris Foote Wood

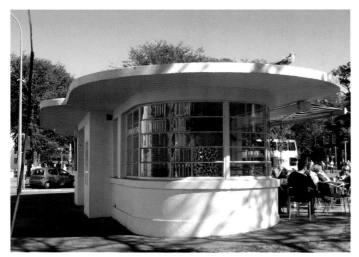

In Brighton's Old Steine, even the deli-café Frankinsteine (Frank in Steine, geddit?) shows its Art Deco influence.

Atlantic Bar & Diner, Castleton Boulevard, Skegness

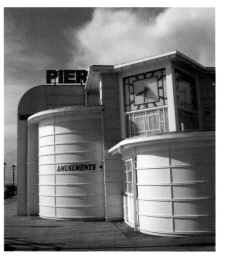

Worthing Pier

The Marlborough, 69 Sea Road, Boscombe

Homage to a great man: Van Alen Building, Marine Parade, Brighton

Marine Court, St Leonards

The Chrysler Building

The Chrysler Building: this 135cm (53in) high, 1:250 scale model of William Van Alen's Art Deco masterpiece was commissioned for the 100-day exhibition, EXPO 98. It was built in perspex and stainless steel from photographs and copies of original blueprints by model-maker Michael Dunk, proprietor of A D Modelmaking.

Model & photos by Michael Dunk

Model

Detail

Entrance

Chapter Three

The Grand Tour

Arriving at the main gate of Tindale Towers, you buzz. Unbeknown to the first-time visitor, this alerts all the phones in the house, every one of which has a gate-release button. In fact, the house – or rather mansion - is so big that owner Mike Keen and his family have taken to using their mobile phones to keep in touch, rather than go on safari to find someone. The gate slides open and you approach the house along a curved driveway. The first thing that strikes you about the garden is that it could be in the South of France. There are palm

trees, for heaven's sake! But with global warming, why not?

You can enter the house through the French windows that open out onto the garden, or go up the access ramp at the back of the house which leads to the garages and parking area on the first floor. There is a separate exit ramp for cars on the north side, allowing a "one-way" traffic system in and out of the Towers.

The ground floor of Tindale Towers is for entertainment. There's the kidney-shaped swimming pool, with hot tub and open shower close by and the steam-room to hand. The tiles that cover the floor and walls of the pool have a blue sheen that captures the light and reflects it from under the water – remarkable! From the pool you go straight into the bar, fully equipped with enough pumps and optics for a medium-sized pub. This also opens up to the garden, and

Palm Trees

South-West aspect

South-East aspect

West aspect

Pool

Garage

Kitchen

Bar

Bar sign

Emma's Room

The other pool room

Adam's Room

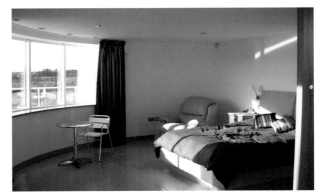

James's Room

there's a 92-inch flat screen dominating one wall for tv, films and videos. Round the back of the bar there's another pool room, this for the ball-and-cue aficionados with plenty of elbow room around the table.

Every grand house has to have a grand staircase, and Tindale Towers is no exception. In this case it's a modern, spiral staircase that goes all the way up to the top of Mike's mansion. The staircase, by the way, is the only place in the house with a carpet.

All the floors throughout Tindale Towers are limestone floors. This is because the underfloor heating, delivered throughout by means of a network of hot-water pipes, would be inhibited by a layer of carpet. Add to that, the advantage of not having to hoover. This fits in with Mike's idea of having a "low maintenance" house, by which he means that repetitive housework should be kept to a minimum. The walls are painted – there's not a scrap of wallpaper anywhere – and the door surrounds and skirting-boards are all in plain, lacquered oak.

The first floor is the "living" floor with its huge kitchen, a large lounge and very roomy cloakrooms. The kitchen occupies the south-west corner, the position in the house with the best views, across the fields to the wooded hill of Brusselton. The Roman Road to Binchester Fort and on to Ebchester and Hadrian's Wall passes this way, as does the

Master sitting room

Master dressing-room

Stair light

Utility room

Stairwell

Top of the stairs

original route of George Stephenson's 1825 Stockton & Darlington Railway. There are three double garages on the first floor, housing various cars and Mike's beloved motorbike, a 1996 1340cc Harley Davidson Cruiser.

The second floor is devoted to four bedroom suites, one for each of Mike's three children and one for guests. Each bedroom suite has its own bathroom, dressing-room and walk-in wardrobe. Every bathroom has a "sun shower" tanning device so you can shower and tan in the one place.

The top floor is reserved for the master and mistress of the house, as it were. There's the master bedroom with its huge balcony, facing south and west. This is the place to watch the sun setting behind Brusselton. There's a fully-equipped private office where Mike and his partner Jules can work from home.

Rather than air conditioning, Tindale Towers has a comprehensive air filtration system that expels the used air which warms the fresh air coming in. Best of all, the system is absolutely silent.

Mike Keen loves Art Deco and was determined that the design of Tindale Towers should be based on this pure and simple concept, which in this case has been developed into a more modernistic style rather than simply replicating what was done in the 1920s and 30s. But Mike can also laugh at himself. "Tindale Towers? I say it's Spanish villa meets Beverley Hills in Bishop Auckland," he jokes.

Sun Room

Master bathroom

Photographs by Peter Davies

Chapter Four

PlanArch Design

Turning the dream into reality

Mike Keen had this great idea to knock down his bungalow and build a house, a fine house, a grand house, a modern house, a real family home. Mike was inspired by the beach houses he had seen in Florida and the South of France, particularly those built on Art Deco principles. Thanks to hard work, astute business dealings and a fair slice of luck, Mike had the funds to have a house built to his own, very particular requirements. All he needed was an architect; someone to draw up the plans, get planning permission and supervise the construction of his dream home: three steps to heaven, easy!

As it happened, Bishop-Auckland based PlanArch Design had already done some work for Mike with the conversion of a former clothing factory for his expanding furniture business. Mike met with PlanArch director John Lavender and designer Colling Morris, and Tindale Towers started to become a reality. It was July 2004. Colling drew up a one-page brief, Mike approved, and the job was under way. "While Mike was very specific about the style he wanted for Tindale Towers, within that he more or less gave us carte blanche to come up with a specific design," said Colling, "I researched many house styles, starting with Le Corbusier and Frank Lloyd Wright."

Examples of the work of these massively-influential architects Colling looked at included Le Corbusier's Villa Savoie (1929-31), a weekend country house in France, and Frank Lloyd Wright's "Fallingwater"

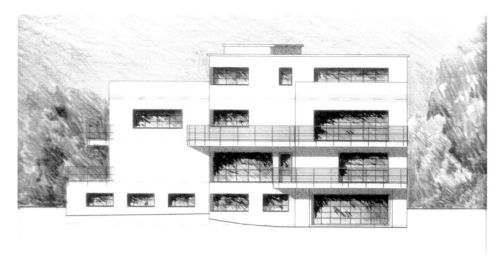

Initial sketch

(1934-37), a vacation house for the wealthy Kaufmann family of Pittsburg, Pennsylvania. Fallingwater has been hailed as "the most famous residence ever built." Tindale Towers, perhaps to be the most famous house in South-West Durham, was to be a modern house, inspired by Art Deco but very much a unique creation.

Colling – his first name, originally a surname, has been used as a middle name in his family for several generations – was inspired as a young boy by pictures of the Eiffel Tower and the Empire State Building. They were in a book at home, and young Colling found himself drawn to look at them time and time again. Born in the Durham hill-top village of Tow Law and now living in nearby Teesdale, Colling is a local lad with a talent for design and a vision well beyond the confines of the home patch he clearly loves.

The next stage was to draw up floor plans. Mike had a clear idea of what he wanted for each floor: leisure and entertaining on the ground floor, kitchen and living rooms on the first floor, bedroom suites for each of his three children on the second floor, and the master bedroom, lounge and private office on the top floor for

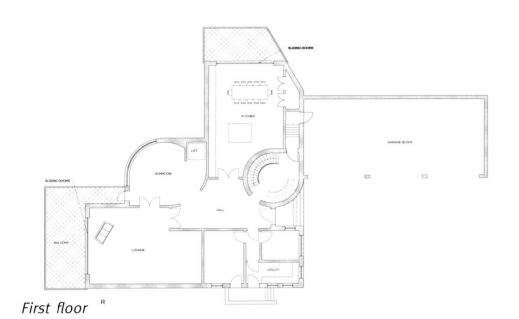

First floor ^R

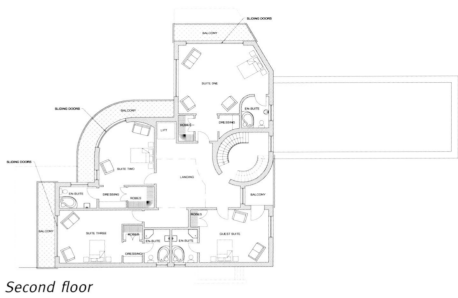

Second floor

Ground floor

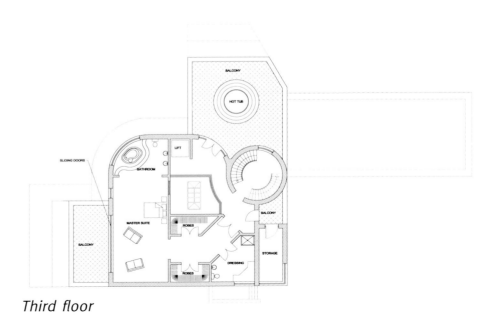

Third floor

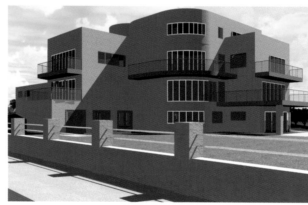

Sketches, plans and models by PlanArch Design

Mike and his partner Jules. It was decided that at the heart of the building there would be a circular staircase tower, connecting all four floors. Every grand house needs a grand staircase, and Tindale Towers is no exception. The top of the staircase tower is glazed to give natural light at the centre of the house, right down through to the bottom floor. This "light well" is a focal point both inside and outside the building. Natural light was a key issue in the design of the building, which resulted in large areas of glazing to many of the rooms. Mike also specified that every room on the upper floors must have a balcony. The views over the Durham countryside had to be there for everyone wherever they were in the house.

There was one design issue between Mike and PlanArch regarding the elevations of Tindale Towers. Colling's original sketches show high-level horizontal banding on the external walls, horizontal glazing bars and railings around the balconies. Mike felt that the horizontal glazing bars would impede the views and it was decided to remove them from the scheme. At the end of the day, Mike was the client and he had the final say. The proposed banding was deleted and the railings replaced with clear glass screens. The result is a building with supremely clean, modern lines.

The next step was to get planning permission. This could have been tricky. Tindale Towers was clearly something quite unusual in a traditional County Durham market town surrounded by pit villages with their rows of terraced miners' cottages. An unusual and thoroughly modern house, a large building in a prominent place on the edge of the town, pristine white and visible for miles around, could well have raised doubts in the minds of the local councillors who constituted Wear Valley District Council's planning committee. But it didn't. Thanks to the presentational skills of Colling Morris and John Lavender – himself a former council planner – the support of the planning department and the perhaps surprisingly enlightened views of the councillors themselves, the plans for Tindale Towers were approved without dissent. After all, these were the same councillors who had given their blessing to a brand-new Georgian mansion, based on original 18th century plans, by erstwhile multi-millionaire and former safe-breaker George Reynolds in the village of Witton le Wear. If a "new" Georgian mansion, why not a New Art Deco mansion?

With planning permission gained, building regulations drawings were commenced, followed by a package of working drawings and specifications to enable what was envisaged to be a traditional tender process to be undertaken. Although the tender process was instigated, it was quickly determined by Mike that his preferred route to procure his dream home was to directly appoint a local construction firm, the directors of which live in Bishop Auckland, and thus Arran Construction of Darlington became the main contractors for the project which was very quickly up and running. During the construction phase, technologist Aaron Cowen and architect Richard Mullen took on the roles of seeing the house come to reality.

At the end of the job comes the "snagging list", all the things that need to be attended to complete the job in every detail. This involves a comprehensive "walk through" of the building noting any defects or problems on the way. This is then passed to the client and contractor for rectification before the official handover takes place. The contractors get their final payment and then, and only then, can Mike Keen relax in his new home, the "house that Mike (*) built."

"Mike Keen's house is a good example of what PlanArch Design is about as a professional practice", said John Lavender. "We have the complementary areas of expertise in planning and architecture under one roof, and we are delighted to provide clients with a quality service on what would be regarded as more conventional planning and architectural projects. However, Mike's house is anything but the conventional project! This was a scheme which required thinking 'outside the box'; a sensitive approach to the planning issues raised, in building a rapport with the Council's planning offices and presenting the house as a positive design statement, at a gateway to Bishop Auckland, to the members of the planning committee.

"Thereafter, the detailed design and construction phase was both exciting and challenging, particularly given the drive, energy and enthusiasm of the client to see his dream translated from drawings and words into reality. This practice is structured to take an initial brief from a client; translate the picture from the client's mind into planning proposals; negotiate the planning process; detail and specify the construction design and materials; and deliver a finished project to the client's satisfaction; all from committed professionals working as one team in the interests of the client and a quality service."

(*) plus at least 300 other people!

PlanArch Design Ltd
Kingsway Court
54 Kingsway
Bishop Auckland
Co. Durham DL14 7JF
Tel: 01388 608 166
Fax: 01388 608 168
Email: e-mail@planarchdesign.co.uk
Web: www.planarchdesign.co.uk

Chapter Five

BDN

Structural design

As soon as structural engineer Clive Oliphant saw the Architectural concept drawings for Tindale Towers, he realised that it would be like no other domestic property that he had ever been asked to design. It soon became clear that Mike Keen was a most unusual client. "We submitted our fee quotation that was accepted immediately and was in fact paid in full when we submitted our first interim invoice," said Clive, "an unusual client indeed!"

Not only is Mike Keen an unusual client, Clive Oliphant is a rare professional who not only does a first-class professional job, but is also ready, willing and able to explain what he does in simple language. Clive describes the design process thus:

"The ground conditions revealed in the extensive Site Investigation report complicated an already difficult design. The use of driven piles was the only practical solution. The foundations were further complicated by the desire to have a swimming pool at basement level, together with the associated ductwork. The need for integral retaining walls pointed to the use of a raft slab sculptured to suit the pool envelope, and service distribution supported on the network of driven piles.

"As with all clients, we and the Architect were working to a changing brief. The difficulty for the Structural Engineer is that, in order to meet a difficult construction programme, the foundation construction

Low-impact office building: Rivergreen Centre, Durham

and hence design needed to be completed ahead of the superstructure final design. Again it became clear that the complex and changing layout did not have sufficient coincident internal walls to form a stiff masonry load-bearing structure. We therefore adopted the design for a steel skeleton frame supporting the floors roof and internal walls, coupled with solid, load-bearing masonry elements where possible.

"The floor-to-floor zones were extremely tight, requiring the extensive use of shallow beams and shelf angles. For acoustic and stability reasons, the floors were generally constructed from pre-cast, pre-stressed planks. However, the complex geometry and the very large cantilever balconies required the extensive use of in-situ reinforced concrete. The roof structure was formed in a similar manner, with local strengthening to support the roof-top jacuzzi. Design changes to move the jacuzzi were asked for too late in the design process and could not be accommodated.

"The property contains a lift serving all the floors. This is again uncommon in a domestic single property, but did not create any structural challenges. However, the other means of vertical travel created significant design challenges as it involved the construction of a four-storey, tightly-wound spiral staircase with no internal support and a sweeping line. Again, in-situ reinforced concrete was used, with cantilever elements to form the landings and enclosing walls.

"The challenges of the scheme did not end with the house. There was the need to accommodate a large basement plant room, four-metre high retaining walls, and a large, open-plan garage. We hope that the structural solutions have complemented the architectural and client aspirations on what was the most challenging domestic single-occupancy scheme we have ever encountered."

Clive Oliphant works in a building he designed, the Rivergreen Centre near Durham City. Clive did the structural and civil engineering design. There, the challenge was to design an environmentally sensitive, low-impact building to provide high specification, modern office accommodation. Equally important in the design process was to create a dramatically pleasing building and a healthy place in which to work.

As far as possible, natural products and sustainable sources were used, reducing air miles and CO_2 emissions. A key to the design was to minimize energy use, water, waste and power while maximizing thermal performance and biodiversity. On a greenfield site bordered by green-belt land and in a prominent position visible from the centre of Durham City, the Rivergreen Centre was restricted to a height of nine metres – two stories. To maximize daylight and natural ventilation, the centre was built to a cruciform plan. Each of the four arms is relatively narrow, at 13 metres, so desks are never more than 6.5 metres from daylight and fresh air.

Rivergreen Centre

The Rivergreen Centre is designed for multi-occupation with offices for up to 100 people in each "arm" – maximum 300 in total. The site is within walking distance of Durham railway station and local bus routes. It's also on the cycle routes. Not only is there a big bike shed, there are showers and a drying room – necessary adjuncts to regular cycling to work. Needless to say, all the waste from the building is sorted and recycled whenever possible. Even the ash from the wood-burning boilers is collected and spread around the flowering trees and shrubs.

Clive Oliphant

Clive Oliphant
BDN Ltd (Durham)
The Rivergreen Centre
Aykley Heads
Durham DH1 5TS
Tel: +44 (0)191 383 7310
Fax: +44 (0)191 383 7311
Email: mailto:durham@bdnltd.com
Web: http://www.bdnltd.com

Chapter Six

Hazelhurst

Measuring up

When plans for any building or construction project have been drawn up, the question is, how much will it cost? That's where the quantity surveyor comes in. Step forward Brian Stace of Hazelhurst ccs Ltd. A resident of Bishop Auckland, like so many of the people involved in creating Tindale Towers, Brian has been involved with many high value dwellings mainly based on an energy sustainable design brief.

"Tindale Towers has been an excellent project to work on, the client has been exceptional and the contractor adaptable and amenable to change," said Brian, "I was introduced into the project after the substructures and foundations had been completed to provide a probity check on the monthly valuations for the project. I was subsequently involved in financial projections to the completion of the works. The project developed in a manner that a form of partnering was required to progress the construction of the building without the delay of producing tender documents at each stage."

Brian has been a quantity surveyor for 30 years, nine years as an Associate with a private practice. His projects included housing, community centres, industrial office and commercial units, ranging in value from £50,000 to £10m. Brian has a particular interest in projects with a high level of energy efficiency, incorporating ecological sustainability within the construction process, including homes for private individuals. One outstanding example is "David's House" in Monmouth, which is totally energy sustainable. Brian has a BSc in quantity surveying, and is a Member of the Association of Project Safety.

"Hazelhurst directors have come together to provide an efficient, consistent and accurate service to all clients at competitive rates with the use of the latest techniques and information systems," says Brian, "the core expertise of Hazelhurst is our quantity surveying service. Based on traditional skills and expertise within the modern context, we believe the unique qualities of the quantity surveyor in terms of cost control and contract are essential within all projects to ensure a successful financial outcome to projects of all types and size." Hazelhurst has undertaken the role of Planning Supervisor for a range of clients. The practice works in association with a local chartered Quantity Surveyor who has over thirty years experience with local authority and social housing.

Past Projects and Clients:

- Energy sustainable visitor centre, York (£240,000);
- Conversion of Victorian Villa to Community Facility, Ashtree House, Savile Town (£210,000);
- "David's House", energy sustainable house, Monmouth (£200,000);
- Gibson Mill restoration, sustainable visitor centre (£1,500,000);
- 48 flats, Bishop Auckland (£3,250,000);
- 12 energy efficient Holiday Cottages, Northumberland (£500,000);
- 9 barn conversions (£900,000);
- 12 self-build houses, Maltby (£325,000);
- 12 self-build houses, Huddersfield (£325,000);
- 8 energy-efficient houses, York (£1,500,000);

Hazelhurst ccs Ltd
70 Cockton Hill Road
Bishop Auckland
Co. Durham DL14 6DB
Tel: 01388 451 229
Email: brian@hazelhurst.freeserve.co.uk

Chapter Seven

Anthony Walters

Legal Eagle

Anthony Walters' offices in Barrington Chambers, Victoria Avenue, Bishop Auckland, look and feel exactly as you would expect a traditional solicitor's office to look and feel with mahogany and leather furniture – all supplied by Mike Keen! Despite the traditional look, there is nothing old-fashioned about Anthony Walters or his law firm. The man himself has an air of dynamism and modernity, far removed from the traditional image of a solicitor with a practice in a County Durham market town.

When Anthony set up his own practice in 1996, he revamped his offices in traditional style, installing a fine wooden staircase in keeping with this handsome Victorian property close to Bishop Auckland town centre. The decoration and furniture had to be just right, and for the right kind of furniture Anthony turned to Mike Keen. "This is quality replica furniture, just what we needed", says Anthony, proudly sitting at his desk which he points out was hand finished. "Barrington Chambers" certainly looks the part. Anthony has acted for Mike Keen since 1991, including buying the bungalow and land where Tindale Towers now stands.

Anthony was born and brought up in Shildon and went to the town's All Saints School and then to Bishop Auckland Grammar School. Fourteen when his father died, Anthony left school three years later. Unable to follow his original intentions of becoming a teacher, Anthony joined a firm of Solicitors in Sedgefield as a Trainee Legal

Barrington Chambers, Victoria Avenue

Executive. Determined to get on, Anthony took correspondence courses all the way leading to the Law Society finals at Chester College of Law.

After serving his Articles with Sedgefield District Council, Anthony became Assistant District Solicitor, entering into private practice in 1983 as a partner with John Hardesty forming the law firm of Hardesty & Walters. Anthony concentrated on Property and Commercial Law and was Chairman of the Bishop Auckland Chamber of Trade for three years. In 1996, at a time when other Solicitors were seeking Legal Aid franchises, Anthony and nine of the Staff set up the current firm which is now recognised as the local firm specialising in Commercial Law but also covering other areas such as Conveyancing, Wills, Family, Personal Injury and Employment.

Ground floor Reception Area

The Board Room

Stairs from Reception

Anthony recognises the importance of good staff, now employing 17, including Solicitors and Legal Executives, specialising in their own fields. Staff turnover is almost non-existent – some of the staff have been with him for over 20 years. This has resulted in clients, who are incredibly loyal, knowing with confidence "who deals with what".

The firm refuses to take on work unless Anthony is confident that he can provide a first-class service. He is a firm believer in networking and often has work referred to him by other firms of Solicitors on a reciprocal basis. If a client wants advice in areas outside the firm's field of expertise Anthony has many contacts with the large firms in Newcastle – he has no fears of referring work to those specialists, knowing full well that the clients will come back to his "Team."

He is very proud of his staff and says: "We are a team of people who have worked together for many years. We are dedicated, enthusiastic and firm believers in the 'team approach.' We are fully computerised with the latest network equipment for accounts, time recording and practice management. Now more than ever it is important to invest in the most up-to-date technology."

Anthony is a Director and current Chairman of the Enterprise Agency for Wear Valley & Teesdale which gives him the opportunity to refer clients to a wide range of business advisers – "If I don't know the answer, I'll know someone who does!" Anthony Walters & Company is a true family firm. He now acts for the children of clients he acted for in 1983, and his two daughters work within the firm. Beth is the receptionist and Catherine is a trainee. "It's great – between 9am and 5.15pm my daughters do what I say – after that it's a different story!" says Anthony.

Head of Practice, Anthony Walters

Anthony Walters & Company
Barrington Chambers
23a Victoria Avenue
Bishop Auckland
Co. Durham DL14 7NE
Tel: 01388 662222
Fax: 01388 450603
DX 60157 Bishop Auckland
Email: aw@anthonywalters.co.uk

Chapter Eight

A house that big? Must be some mistake!

Arran Construction built Tindale Towers. Of course, many other companies and individuals were involved, but Arran were the main contractors and are justifiably proud of this most unusual job. In line with Mike Keen's philosophy, Arran are a local firm, and in line with Mike Keen's philosophy, Arran were instructed to use local firms as subcontractors whenever possible. Like Mike, Arran itself has deep local roots.

In the 1960s and 70s, the building and construction firm of G Stephenson & Son was the biggest employer in Bishop Auckland, with a workforce of 650 at its peak and "big enough to float on the Stock Exchange," according to Arran boss Dave Lee. The driving force of the company was Harold Stephenson, son of the founder. A big man in more ways than one, Harold built up the family business from a small, six-man joinery & undertakers business into a vast undertaking that did major building and civil engineering work throughout Northern England. Harold was also a big man on the local council and Chairman of the Bishop Auckland UDC Works Committee. When he died, hundreds attended his funeral.

While his father was reputed to have started with a horse and cart, Harold had not one but two Rolls Royces. "It's the only car I'm comfortable in," was his excuse, not that he needed one. Nobody begrudged Harold his wealth – he'd earned it, and he gave generously to local causes. One Rolls he used for everyday business, while his Rolls Corniche was his pleasure drive. In those days, a job

Gaunt frame

with "Stivvies" was a job for life. Dave Lee joined the firm at eighteen, straight from school. That was 1963, but by the mid-1980s Harold had died and the firm was in trouble. In 1985 G Stephenson & Son went into liquidation and Lee – along with the rest of the Stephenson workforce – was out of a job.

"It was a shock, being faced with the dole after twenty-odd years with the same company," said Lee, "while redundancy is traumatic, it did motivate latent desires for self-employment. So the four of us got together to form our own company." And so Arran Construction (Bishop Auckland) Ltd was created. The "four of us" were Lee, Tony Williams, Dave Trotter and Gordon Holden. Lee had been Stephenson's chief quantity surveyor, Williams the chief designer, Trotter was a site foreman and Holden a planner. Lee and Williams were the first directors, Trotter and Holden also becoming directors when Williams retired. The name "Arran" was chosen simply to be at the start of Yellow Pages. Bishop Auckland was added to avoid duplication at Companies House.

Arran's first job was one they took over from Stephensons, and goodwill with employers gained them further work. Arran recruited their workforce from men they knew, but the key factor in the new company's success was to make their site managers shareholders. "You're only as good as the man on site," says Lee, "having a stake in the business is the best possible motivation." In the early years Arran had no offices and the managers worked from home, often having to change from dirty workclothes, shower and don suit and briefcase before going on to a business meeting. But Arran decided from the start that they would stay "lean and mean." Having observed the problems at Stephensons, Arran's policy has been to repay borrowings quickly to remove bank restraints. They also decided not to have a builder's yard and to hire in mechanical plant instead of buying it.

Arran expanded, providing a design-and-build service for steel-framed industrial buildings as a Ward Atlas System "preferred contractor." The company now employs 16-18 core staff, plus sub-contractors, and has a £2.5m a year turnover. Having made a policy decision that they would not get into the business of building houses (or "house-bashing", as Dave Lee puts it), Arran almost missed the chance to build Tindale Towers. Lee takes up the story.

"I came into the office one day to find one of those little yellow 'post-it' notes on my desk, asking if we could tender for a 9,000 sq ft house. We'd put up factories smaller than that, so I thought it must be a mistake. I guessed it was for a 900 sq ft house, not something we would be interested in, so I binned it! Anyway, some days later I got a call to go and see Mike Keen at his furniture works. The rest, as they say, is history."

Bare site

Setting out

On the level – Mike Keen's old bungalow (now demolished)

First frame

With such a complex job, the construction work was divided into three separate contracts: groundworks, superstructure and fitting out. Mechanical and electrical work was sub-let to specialist contractors on a design-and-build basis to fit in with the particular requirements of the job - and the client. The groundworks alone involved driving 181 piles, each 17 metres long. Ground conditions were "appalling." The site had originally been clay pits for the Shaw Knight company who made pipes and sanitary ware. To get down to the solid clay strata underneath, hundreds of tonnes of poor and mixed landfill had to be relocated for separation and returned as suitable fill for recycling around the building. Needless to say, building Tindale Tower took several months longer than originally envisaged.

Tindale Towers is very much a unique and individual building, and getting it built raised far more than the usual problems involved in a multi-million pound construction. Constant site meetings, onerous health and safety requirements, making everything fit together in time and space, plus the particular requirements of Mike Keen as a client with clear ideas of what he does and doesn't want, made it a major test for all involved. Remarkably, Mike in effect became a member of the workforce, both for design and construction. This could have been a nightmare for the architects and builders, but not so. Dave Lee again:

"A particular feature of this project was the increasing time spent by the client on site and his interest and grasp of the particular trades, problems and resolutions. This 'hands on' approach by the client, from selection of materials to use of local sub-contractors, has led to a 'Mike wants' culture from professional advisors all the way through to site workmen. Mike was on site every day, often twice a day. Unusually for a client, he made it his business to get to know everything that was going on. He talked to the workmen, and had a better grasp of each individual trade than some professionals. Whenever there was a problem, as there often was, Mike would always take a positive attitude of how to get things sorted out.

Steelfixers show their skills

First floor fix

First lift bricks

First floor goes in

Where?

Anticipating the view

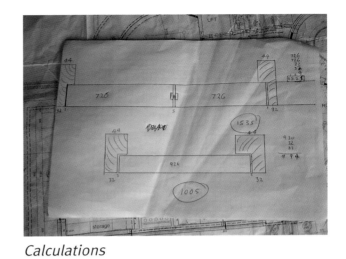

Calculations

Complicated pipework

Not long to go

Nearly finished

Pictures by PlanArch Design

"As our contractual agreements evolved, it became clear that the client was a rare species and understood that contractors are more than willing to give value for money, provided cash flow problems could be resolved. I'm not just saying this, but for us Mike Keen has been the perfect client."

The Arran directors' "pen pictures" of themselves: Dave Lee: physical wreck, past his "sell-by" date; has been going to retire next year for the last three years; qualified ARICS and M. Inst. C.E.S. as a quantity surveyor; spends more time estimating and general management than quantity surveying; likes: big desk, big seat and avoiding telephone disturbances; habitat: butterfly, only outside when warm and sunny; role: obtaining work and ensuring reward for the effort.

Dave Trotter: was tradesman joiner, his potential to site management identified early from former company (Stephensons); invited to join Arran as the best of the "young" foremen; now has wealth of site experience; even-tempered, copes under pressure, communicates well with clients and advisors; likes: gardening; could have been a smallholder if the rewards had been acceptable; role: working with client and designers to find practical methods of achieving designed ideas.

Gordon Holden: intermittent supervisor in Dave Trotter's absence; "hands on" achiever; far too fit, works all week and cycles for pleasure (in figure-hugging Lycra and sun-shades!).

Arran Construction's Three Merry Men (l-r): Dave Trotter, Gordon Holden, Dave Lee

Chris Foote Wood

Arran Construction Ltd
Cleveland Hall
Cleveland Street
Darlington
Co. Durham DL1 2PE
Tel: 01325 463 166
Email: enquiries@arranconstruction.co.uk

Chapter Nine

Priory Safety Services

Health & Safety

Health and safety has always been an essential aspect of any construction project, now more than ever. With so many different trades, contractors and sub-contractors involved in a large and complex building like Tindale Towers, having a single organization to take responsibility for ensuring safe working on site is a must. Such an individual, unique building must also be designed with safety in mind for the family who are to live there and anyone visiting.

For this crucial job, Mike Keen turned to Priority Safety Services of Tynemouth and its managing director Michael Bayley. Catching Michael for a brief interview, he said: "when Mike asked me to help him with the Tindale Towers project, I was more than happy to oblige. Having undertaken work for Mike in the past, I found him to be someone who was not only approachable but easy to talk to. The structure designed by Mike and PlanArch Design was clearly going to be thought-provoking in terms of health and safety, but having worked on a similar scheme it was something I knew a bit about.

"The secret of planning any project in terms of health and safety is to 'get in at the beginning,' and that is exactly what I did. I had various meetings with architects Richard Mullen and Aaron Cowen of PlanArch, plus of course Mike himself, to ensure that the planned structure was not only going to be feasible to be built but was also going to be a house that one could live in safely. This concept of forward thinking is something Priory Safety Services is keen to instil into all its clients and we actively encourage as much dialogue as possible with all organisations right from the start of any project.

"As the Planning Supervisor on the scheme (a position that is now abolished to make way for the new CDM* Co-ordinator) I took an active role in attending progress meetings. I also visited the site to ensure that should any changes be suggested they were feasible for the contactor to undertake in terms of the health and safety of his employees on site and that of Mike and his family when the building work had ended. *Construction Design & Management – not Cadbury's Dairy Milk! CFW

"Now that the project is complete and the vision Mike had two years ago has been achieved I am more than pleased I have been able to help. The team of experts Mike has used have been first class and anyone wanting to develop a similar scheme should look no further than PlanArch Design. Naturally, we would hope that they would also look to Priory Safety Services to assist them with the project's health and safety issues.

"Tindale Towers is a Grand Design and should be viewed by as many people in the building trade as possible to see what can be achieved by careful planning."

Priory Safety Services Limited is an independent consultancy offering advice and assistance on a wide range of health and safety topics. The Company's managing director is Michael Bayley MBA, CMIOSH, DipSHEM, MaPS. Details of Priory's services can be found on their website www.priory-safety-services.co.uk or by contacting their office on 0191 270 8070.

Priory Safety Services Ltd
1 The Drive
Tynemouth NE30 4JP
Tel: 0191 270 8070
Email: michael@priory-safety-services.co.uk

"No swearing or blaspheming" – Mike Bayley of Priory Safety Services at his desk.

Chris Foote Wood

Chapter Ten

Roger Bullivant

Piling in

Driving the piles

Firm foundations are essential for any building. For better or worse, Mike Keen decided to construct his extensive, four-storey New Art Deco mansion on what was very poor ground. This is, after all, the flood-plain of the River Gaunless. The ground next to Mike's bungalow – demolished to make way for TT (Tindale Towers) - consisted of a filled-in former clay pit with a mixture of clay, sand and silt underneath. The solution was to sink piles through these layers, down to a bearing strata, and to build a concrete platform on which TT now stands.

Roger Bullivant Limited, the largest foundations engineering company in the UK, was the first major sub-contractor to be brought in, in October 2005. In the remarkably short time of ten days, the Roger Bullivant site team with their powerful piling rig sank no fewer than 181 pre-cast reinforced concrete piles, each approximately eight inches square in section, to an average depth of 17.17 metres (56ft). Just two piles broke during driving and were replaced. There was a brief hold-up while Mike's bungalow was demolished – that took only a day – before piling resumed.

The ground conditions were established by surveys carried out in early 2005. These included drilling three boreholes to a depth of twelve metres (39ft), and digging nine trial pits with an average depth of 4.6m (15ft). The results were perhaps even worse than had been expected. The whole of the site is "made ground", that is, loose material of all kinds which has been used to fill the former clay pit, also known as a "borrow" pit, and to cover the whole area. The strata for quite a depth below the surface is of very poor material. The River Gaunless lies only 160m to the south of the site, and over the millennia it has deposited sand and silt over the valley floor – a typical flood plain now guarded by an extensive flood protection scheme.

After the site had been cleared and levelled, the "footprint" of TT was set out and the position of each pile marked. When all 181 concrete piles had been driven down to the bearing strata, the tops were cropped and the reinforced concrete slab laid on top. The steel reinforcing bars of the piles and of the base slab were welded together before the concrete for the floor was poured in and set. This has provided TT with the firmest and strongest possible base.

RB Quiet Hammer

Roger Bullivant

Established in 1971 by the present Chairman Roger Bullivant, as a specialist civil and structural engineering company, the Roger Bullivant Group has grown into the largest foundation company in the UK. With an annual turnover in excess of £110m, the company offers an extensive range of quality foundation products and pre-cast solutions. RB offers value engineered solutions in Piling, Mini-Piling, Ground Improvement, House Foundations, Underpinning, Special Pre-cast Concrete Products, Geothermal Heating and Conservatory and Extension Bases.

From the early days when RB began in small diameter mini-piling, the Group has expanded into all aspects of piling and onward into the provision of complete design and construct foundation packages. All specialised plant and equipment is designed and built "in-house" at the company's 250-acre manufacturing headquarters site in Burton-on-Trent. The company also has two other manufacturing facilities in the UK and seven other specialist centres. Roger Bullivant Ltd wholeheartedly embraces the philosophy of off-site, factory-based prefabrication.

The RB range of over 80 pile and mini-pile types encompasses both displacement and replacement piles. Displacement piles can be provided in traditional forms such as driven pre-cast concrete, driven steel tubes or timber, driven and vibrated cast in-situ or displacement auger techniques (continuous helical displacement). The portfolio of replacement piles includes CFA (continuous flight auger) and open hole augered piles. Nowadays, displacement piles are increasing in popularity as no arisings are brought to the surface and there is therefore no material to remove from site.

To promote the company's skills and educate the construction professional the RB Marketing Department organises a year round range of seminars and conferences including the RB Breakfast Club which offers professionals a free full monty breakfast whilst listening to a CPD accredited presentation. The full schedule of events can be found at events@roger-bullivant.co.uk

Cleared site

Piledriving rig

Pictures by PlanArch Design

Tindale Towers piling contract:
No of piles: 181
Type & size of piles: precast reinforced concrete, 200x200mm (8x8in)
Average length of piles: 17.17m (56ft)
No of replacement piles: 2

Roger Bullivant accreditations, affiliations and standards awards:
- BBA (British Board of Agrément) designated by Government to issue technical approval to innovative products for which no industry standard applies.
- BSI (British Standards Institute) official Approval of Production Quality Standards CARES (Certification Authority for Reinforcing Systems) providers of Quality Assurance accreditation for the production of pre-cast concrete beam.
- FPS (Federation of Piling Specialists) professional Trade Organisation for the Piling Industry.
- ASUC (Association of Specialist Underpinning Contractors) professional Trade Organisation of Underpinning Contractors
- DFI (Deep Foundation Institute) International Trade Association for Foundations.

Roger Bullivant Ltd
Walton Road,
Drakelow,
Burton-on-Trent,
Staffordshire DE15 9UA
Tel: 01283 511115
Fax: 01283 512233
Email: marketing@roger-bullivant.co.uk
Web: www.roger-bullivant.co.uk

- 43 -

Chapter Eleven

Tomlinson-Longstaff

Power play

Behind the many lights/switches and electrical equipment in Tindale Towers lie miles of electrical cabling and hundreds of items of electrical equipment. Due to the sheer size and hi-specification of the property, the electrical installation needed to be carried out by a company with a wealth of knowledge and experience. The company chosen to complete this was Tomlinson Longstaff Ltd, a local business with decades of dedicated commitment, gaining them the expertise of electrical installations.

Tomlinson-Longstaff Ltd was established in 1973 by two founder members called – guess what? – Tomlinson and Longstaff. Doug Tomlinson and David Longstaff were both local qualified electricians. They were working for a local business of electrical contractors, and decided to embark on creating their own business. Sadly, both Doug and David have passed away, but the business they created over thirty years ago is firmly established in the market place and is still going strong employing around thirty employees. Foreman electrician Mark Woods, grandson of founder Doug Tomlinson, is a long-serving employee and worked on the Tindale Towers contract from start to finish.

Tomlinson Longstaff is now solely owned by Managing Director Tony Kirkup who originally bought into the company in March 1995. Tony has expanded the business greatly over the years with his expertise

Electricians Kelvin Smith (left) and Mark Woods

(l-r): Trevor Edwards (contracts manager), Mark Woods (foreman electrician), Tony Kirkup (managing director)

in the Electrical Contracting Industry driving the Company forward from strength to strength. Trevor Edwards is the contracts manager and Jill O'Hare is the company secretary, all the office staff working as a team, Angela Kirkup, Sharon Jackson, and Alicia Manners. The company is still at its original location in West Auckland making it practical geographically, most the company's employees live within a few miles radius, however the premises have recently been tastefully refurbished. The main office is the nerve centre of the business with a hive of activity where everyone keeps in close communication to drive the business forward.

The company offers a complete professional service at competitive rates. Quotations are provided free and without obligation. Tomlinson-Longstaff are members of and approved by NICEIC (National Inspection Council of Electrical Installation Contracting). NICEIC is the industry's independent body, set up to protect consumers against unsafe and unsound electrical installations. T-L undertake all types of electrical work, both commercial and industrial, and has won contracts for schools throughout the North East and refurbishments of stately Hotels throughout England, working to full specification.

Working with main contractors Arran Construction, Tomlinson-Longstaff have carried out the full electrical installation at Tindale Towers, including the main distribution, small power and emergency lighting. With lots of electrical equipment all around the house and a lift, and supplying power to such things as remotely-controlled curtains and entry gates, this extensive and complicated contract has involved a huge amount and variety of electrical work.

The wide selection of services provided by Tomlinson-Longstaff are:-

- Complete design
- Installation lighting
- Consultancy
- Rewiring
- Refurbishments
- Electrical installation testing
- Inspection fault diagnosis
- Portable appliance testing
- Fire alarm installations, including projects for Honeywell Gents, leading specialists in the UK
- Door entry systems
- Emergency lighting

(l-r): Trevor, Tony, Mark admire their work

National Inspection Council for
Electrical Installation Contracting

APPROVED CONTRACTOR

Photos by Chris Foote Wood

Chapter Twelve

Gilwood Engineering

Grey water, green heat

The Tindale Towers heating system designed and installed by Gilwood Engineering of North Shields employs the latest green technology. For example, heat exchangers ensure that the fresh air coming into the building from outside is warmed by the stale air being expelled from the rooms by heat recovery units. Rainwater from the roof, collected and stored in an underground tank, is first filtered and then pumped back up and used to flush Tindale Towers' numerous toilets. This is called "grey water" and saves using treated drinking water – which is metered, by the way – thus cutting down water bills.

The house is warmed throughout by an underfloor heating system which is served by warm-water pumped through pipes which are set in a screed on top of insulation board. As carpet underlay would act as an insulating layer, all the floors in the house are laid with stone tiles. Add to that the hot water system to serve all of the bathrooms, and there is a lot of heating to do. All this is achieved by three state-of-the-art Zenex gas-fired boilers which don't look like boilers at all. Each comes in its own self-contained unit 750mm square and two metres tall, looking rather like a telephone box. These boilers live in the plant room, which is the pride and joy of Gilwood's installation supervisor Bill Joynes.

Bill and his henchmen, plumbers Dave Cross and Alan Kenny, plus apprentice Phil Cornes, know the innards of Tindale Towers – intimately. Their job was to install the hugely complicated heating and plumbing system and get it up and running – essential to making the house not only liveable in but also comfortable and enjoyable to live in. "If we've done our job right, Mike and his family won't even notice the system working," says Bill.

Gilwood also supplied and installed what is delicately called the sanitary ware, the sinks, baths, and – yes – the toilets. With many rooms having their own en-suite facilities, and toilets on every floor, that amounts to a whole lot of sanitary ware. All the toilets and sinks are "wall hung", that is, they are fixed to the wall rather than to the floor. Clearly they have to be strong enough to bear the weight of any heavyweight boxer, rugby player or Japanese sumo wrestler who might be a guest at Tindale Towers.

Fixing Saniware in the poolroom toilet: (l-r) Phil Cornes (apprentice), Bill Joynes (supervisor), Davey Cross (plumber)

Bill and Phil contemplate their work in the penthouse bathroom   Chris Foote Wood

Gilwood undertook the complex task of designing the heating and plumbing system – and costing it – and this was managed by another local lad, local to North Shields that is, Charles Clark. Many years ago, Charles did what a lot of Geordies did and still do – he went to work away to "seek his fortune." Charles gained valuable knowledge and experience working in the Middle East and a number of European countries before returning to the UK to work with Wimpey Construction "Special Projects" division before deciding to set up Gilwood Engineering Services Limited.

The main part of the Tindale Towers project was managed by Tom Millmore who joined Gilwood in 2006 as Director in charge of Mechanical and Plumbing works and has enjoyed the interesting challenges of Tindale Towers. Tom has been ably assisted by Ben Nicholson, originally an engineering apprentice with the company and now developing into a competent Contracts Engineer. Gilwood have encouraged the development and training of its staff and apprentices for many years, a department managed and maintained by Sheila Clark who pays great attention in ensuring her "boys" do their homework for college! Given that the company has won and appeared in many Apprentice of the Year presentations, someone is doing their job right.

Gilwood Engineering are mechanical, electrical and plumbing contractors. Formed

Teacher and pupil – Mark & Adam

Man at work - Ben

Sheila & Bob visit Ben at JJB Sports

Marconi House: luxury apartments in Newcastle

Star apprentice – Adam Lumsden

Apartments in Blyth

in 1985, the company provides a complete "single solution" service for design and installation. Undertaking work from £1,000 to £1m, Gilwood has an impressive list of clients who include Amec, Bowey, Shepherd, Komatsu, Gordon Durham, Sir Robert McAlpine and Newcastle City and North Tyneside Councils.

A recent £700,000 job upgrading bathrooms and kitchens in a 19-storey block of flats in the centre of Newcastle for Kendal Cross Holdings involved installing sanitary ware, above-ground drainage, hot & cold water, general power, lighting, smoke & fire alarms, door entry systems and extract ventilation. Gilwood were the main contractors for a complex £500,000 scheme at York General Hospital which involved the refurbishment of operating theatre areas and the replacement of six different rooftop plant-rooms, as well as installing new air conditioning throughout and are proud to have achieved completion of the work on programme. A major refurbishment of the office buildings for Komatsu was undertaken, with the company managing the whole of the works over two phases. This included providing temporary accommodation for the whole of the design, and buying offices whilst the building and engineering work was taking place.

Master bathroom

Peter Davies

Gilwood Engineering Services Ltd
22 Northumberland Square
North Shields
NE30 1PW
Tel: 0191 214 2616
Fax: 0191 214 2655
Email: cclark@gilwoodmast.co.uk

Chapter Thirteen

Zenex

Energy-saving technology

From its 'Art Deco' concept to its high technical specifications, Tindale Towers building has been both a challenging construction and a source of inspiration for many future designs. Situated in Bishop Auckland, the property has an internal floor area of 1,225sqm. It includes five bathrooms, all with baths and showers, three separate shower rooms and a swimming pool and Jacuzzi with a surface area of 27sqm. Consequently, the building requires a high performance heating and domestic hot water system that is capable of delivering all year round heating for the living areas and the swimming pool, as well as providing hot water for its multiple bathrooms and shower rooms.

Zenex Technologies was commissioned to provide a solution that would ensure the installation maximised energy performance without compromising functionality. In addition, the high efficiency of the system allowed it to be accommodated within a relatively small boiler room.

Zenex Technologies has developed a unique technology known as Cool Flue. This patented technology is incorporated into the GasSaver, a boiler flue attachment that recovers heat from the flue waste combustion gases which are normally lost to the atmosphere and then uses it to pre-heat the domestic hot water. The device is simply installed on top of a gas-fired combination boiler and works by using a flue gas condenser to condense water from the flue

Installing Zenex boilers: Bill and Phil of Gilwood Engineering in the plant room

gasses storing up to six litres. Incoming cold mains water passes through one heat exchanger in this store and another in the flue. Water leaving the store is heated to a temperature as high as 80°C and is then blended with the cold mains water to a temperature of 30°C for entry to the boiler.

Laboratory tests in the UK and Holland have shown that the Zenex GasSaver can reduce the gas used in the production of domestic hot water by 37% on average over the year. In combination with a modern SEDBUK A rated boiler consumers have reported a reduction of up to 50% on their gas bills. For a property the size of Tindale Towers this will represent significant savings.

Three Zenex Boilers in the TT Plant Room

Zenex boilers with their protective screens   Pictures by Chris Foote Wood

With multiple bathrooms and a large swimming pool to heat the domestic water usage at Tindale Towers is expected to be extraordinary. In addition to gas savings, Zenex's GasSaver also provides a water saving solution. Since the GasSaver allows water to be heated and delivered much faster than a standard condensing boiler it cuts down on the normal wastage of lukewarm water running off from the tap when hot water is required. This will result in an important volume of water saved yearly.

Zenex's solution was to install its Blade system. This is a fully self contained heating and/or hot water server which comes in different sizes to meet a diverse range of applications and is housed in a rigid, space efficient enclosure. Each Blade contains a boiler and GasSaver, a cylinder and all interconnecting pipework and electrics. Individual Blade units are plugged together to provide a tailored modular solution.

Thanks to the Blades, the normally wasted energy is recovered through the GasSaver and can be reused to pre-heat either the incoming cold water main or the primary heating circuit. By reclaiming and reusing otherwise wasted energy, the Zenex Blade improves the efficiency of the boiler system to 98%. In addition, there is an optional Energy Recovery Unit (ERU) available, a separate 100 to 250 litre thermal store to further increase the energy recovered from the waste flue gases and that works in conjunction with the Blade units.

To meet Tindale Towers' requirements, the property required two Zenex Xi3 Blades for heating purposes and one Xi1 Blade hot water server.

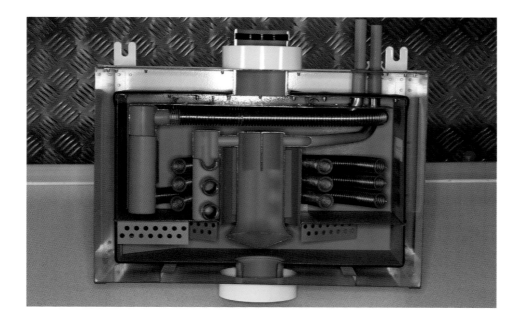

The Xi3 Blades installed in this property supply heating for the entire home including the swimming pool and the underfloor heating. These Blades use a dual GasSaver Energy Recovery Unit on each Blade which recovers 12% of the energy consumed by the heating system and is re-used to provide hot water via the Xi1 Blade. Due to the property size and the swimming pool heating requirements, the amount of energy recovered is expected to be significant.

The Xi1 Blade hot water server delivers all hot water required at Tindale Towers including all bathrooms, shower rooms, sinks and basins. The Xi1 Blade incorporates a single GasSaver Energy Recovery Unit that combined with the recovered energy from the Xi3 Blade results in an overall system efficiency of around 97%.

Chris Farrell, Managing Director of Zenex, comments: "Our GasSaver is an energy efficient solution for any household. It maximises the performance of condensing boilers and helps to reduce gas bills as well as water wastage. However, for a property like Tindale Towers with especially high requirements on heating and domestic hot water systems, Zenex Blades system offered an ultimate energy saving solution recovering wasted energy."

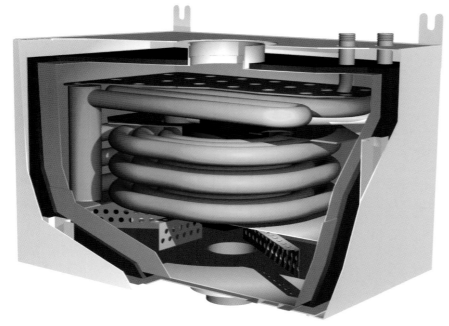

Zenex GasSaver

Zenex Energy Saving Technology
Unit 2 Broadley Park Road
Roborough, Plymouth
Devon PL6 7EZ
Tel: 0800 328 7533
Email: chris@zenexenergy.com
Web: www.zenexenergy.com

Chapter Fourteen

JMW Aluminium

A clear view

One thing that Tindale Towers owner Mike Keen was "keen" on (if you'll excuse the pun) was that the whole aspect of his mansion should be simple, clean and clear, to give his home the shape, form and appearance of classis Art Deco house architecture. That meant straight lines and bold curves, plain walls and clear balustrading. Given its location on the edge of town, looking out over green fields and wooded hills, Mike wanted his TT mansion to make the most of the light and the views.

An integral part of the TT design is the vast space given to floor-to-ceiling windows and glazed doors that open out onto the gardens on the ground floor and the numerous, roomy balconies on the upper floors. At the same time, Mike naturally wanted his home to be wind and weather-proof. So all the glazed units, windows and doors needed to be top quality and expertly fitted. Installing glazed units in curved walls was an additional challenge, taken on by specialist contractors JMW Aluminium of Newcastle.

JMW is named after its founder, John M Wadds. He set up business in Newcastle upon Tyne in 1964, concentrating on 24-hour emergency boarding-up and re-glazing of damaged windows. Incorporation followed in 1971, under the name of John M Wadds (Building and Glazing) Limited, and for the next three decades the company traded highly successfully in this field. In 1987 the company diversified into the field of fabricating and installing architectural aluminium systems

Bedroom view at Tindale Towers   PlanArch Design

nationwide. Since 1997 the company has been known as JMW (Aluminium) Limited and now concentrates its activities solely in the aluminium field.

JMW is proud of its relationship with major players in the construction market. Some of the many projects JMW has been involved with over recent years include Debenhams and the Red Quadrant at the Metro Centre, the Visitor Centre at Alnwick Gardens, the BMW Training Centre at Wokefield Park near Reading, and the development of Newcastle College, Rye Hill Campus.

The company remains based in Newcastle upon Tyne and still has strong family links. Currently JMW employs 45 members of staff and is committed to investing time, energy and money into developing

their skills. All of the site operatives and managers hold CSCS cards to NVQ Level 2 and 3, and all fabricators and trainee fabricators hold NVQ2 in the Fabrication of Glass Supporting Frames. JMW's dedication to staff development was formally recognised in 2005 when the company achieved Investors in People (IiP) status.

JMW predominantly work with the Schuco Aluminium System, as used on the Tindale Towers project. The company also fabricates and installs Technal, Comar, Kawneer, Smart and Senior aluminium systems. JMW's current projects include School PFI Schemes in Gateshead and Newcastle, where they have completed three schools with another three ongoing.

David Mills (on left) and Dean Humphrey install folding doors at TT

Sunburst - external door, first floor   Chris Foote Wood

Station canopy

Offices

Bus station entrance

Newcastle Airport's new Air Traffic Control Centre

Pictures by JMW Aluminium

JMW Aluminium Ltd
Architectural House
Plummer Street
Newcastle upon Tyne NE4 7AB
Tel: 0191-273 3366
Email: TW@jmwaluminium.com
Web: www.jmwaluminium.com

Chapter Fifteen

Evershed Products

Environment-friendly decking

"Think global, act local" is a well-known environmental slogan. Two of the things Mike Keen had in mind in constructing Tindale Towers was for the house to be as "green" as possible and to source materials from the local area if at all possible. These two things came together with local firm Evershed Products providing the decking and gate panels, all made from recycled materials.

There is a double benefit in using Evershed's environment-friendly products. Not only are they made out of recycled materials, they replace the use of timber and so reduce the number of trees to be cut down. In addition, the recycled material – unlike wood - does not need special treatment and regular maintenance, and should last indefinitely.

Amazingly, the raw material Evershed use for all their products – which include fencing, seats and other garden furniture as well as decking – comes from polystyrene and plastic recovered from old CD cases and anything made from polystyrene, eg coffee cups. Instead of filling up scarce landfill space, these redundant items are recycled and the plastic turned into tiny pellets which Evershed buy in by the ton.

On arrival at the factory, Evershed have a huge machine (a bit like something from Willie Wonka's chocolate factory) which mixes the pellets with polymers and turns them into a solid mass which is extruded in the required profile. These long lengths are then cut up

Top Deck

Peter Davies

to make decking, chairs, tables and anything else that is required. While narrow items like fencing can be nailed on, most Evershed products are put together by being drilled and bolted or screwed.

And instead of being painted as with timber products, Evershed's production comes ready-coloured by the simple expedient of putting the required paint colour into the original mix.

After 25 years working for Durham County and Darlington Borough councils in grounds maintenance, local lad Ron Drennan decided to set up his own business. At first he bought in ready-made lengths of recycled material to make up his products, but when that proved too expensive, he invested in his £250,000 machine to make them himself. Ron now employs four staff at his factory on Bishop Auckland's South Church Enterprise Park, no more than half a mile away from Tindale Towers.

The material coming out of the machine needs to be the right density. Too dense, and it will be brittle and crack. Too light, and it will break too easily. While Evershed material can replace wood for most purposes, it cannot be used for load-bearing structures like roof trusses. For tables and chairs, it is fine.

Thanks to the way that they are made, Evershed products are extremely versatile. One speciality is a picnic table with disabled access – room for people in wheelchairs to enjoy a picnic with everyone else. Ron Drennan is particularly proud of the communal area at South Church Allotments, which he provided with seats, benches, planters and pergolas.

Evershed products really do not need any maintenance other than a quick rub-down with soap and water, especially if they are sited under a tree! Evershed proudly claim that their products are environmentally friendly and maintenance-free, do not rot, crack or splinter, and are waterproof, UV stable and impervious to fungal attack(!). There are two different types of material, recycled "high and medium impact" polystyrene, and recycled low density polytheline

The largest area of decking at Tindale Towers is at the top of the building, eight metres by eight. With the other decking and the gate panels, it is the largest single order Ron Drennan has ever had.

Evershed Products
20-22 Nuns Close
South Church Enterprise Park
Co. Durham DL14 6XD
Tel: 01388 777666
Fax: 01388 778666
Email: admin@evershedproducts.co.uk
Web: www.evershedproducts.co.uk

Balcony Deck

PlanArch Design

Top Deck

Peter Davies

Close-up

PlanArch Design

Decking over garden

PlanArch Design

Chapter Sixteen

NYT

Timber!

Going around Tindale Towers, one thing you notice is just how much wood there is. The internal doors, skirting boards and architraves are all wood. And there's the dance floor in the bar. All this timber was supplied by North Yorkshire Timber which in its near 30-year existence has expanded well beyond its Yorkshire base. The local NYT depot is on the outskirts of Darlington a few miles down the road from where TT is located, just outside Bishop Auckland on the Darlington Road.

The distinctive timber used for the TT doors and their surrounds comes from Spanish company Docavi, based at Villacañas near Toledo in central Spain. Other NYT timbers come from other exotic places such as Mexico and El Salvador. But traditional timbers like oak, beech, cherry and pine are much in evidence at NYT.

Buying timber used to be a case of "roughing it" down the local timber yard, in complete contrast to the NYT branches today which are more akin to ultra-modern supermarkets with a similarly huge array of products, materials and designs. There's scarcely a speck of sawdust to be seen. Only the musak and the canned adverts are missing, for which much thanks. Windows, timber decking and natural stone paving are there in abundance.

You can now shop on line for your hardwood flooring and timber doors. NYT has its own dedicated "floors & doors" website – called an E-shop - for those who want to shop from home, or view the products available before visiting.

NYT are FSC (Forest Stewardship Council) accredited timber suppliers, and are committed to protecting the environment through our responsible purchasing policy. The company only purchases from suppliers who are registered with a recognised scheme such as FSC, PEFC (Programme for the Endorsement of Forest Specification) or FPCC (Forest Products Chain of Custody initiative). The Chain of Custody is the timber industry's term for knowing the source of timber, enabling it to be traced from the forest to the end-user. NYT says it has always sourced its timber products from reputable companies. For example, NYT's principle Swedish timber supplier for the past twelve years - Bergkvist - is PEFC registered.

The company has a workforce of 165. Nick Kershaw is sales & marketing director, Paul Wyer is group sales executive and Gordon Bache is the Darlington branch manager. Other NYT branches are at Ripon, Richmond, Middlesbrough, Sunderland (Joseph Thompson Timber) and Wingate in County Durham (Ward & Naylor).

Branch manager Gordon Bache and Andrea Agnew (admin assistant) in one small corner of the NYT showroom.

North Yorkshire Timber
Standard House
Thurston Road
Northallerton Business Park
Northallerton
North Yorks DL6 2NA
Tel: 01609 780 777
Fax: 01609 777 888
Email: sales@nytimber.co.uk
Web: www.nytimber.co.uk
E-shop: www.flooringanddoors.co.uk

Chapter Seventeen

Prices Paving

Tiles that glow in the dark

Go to the Tindale Towers pool at night, and you'll se an amazing sight – tiles that glow in the dark! The pillars, and the pool walls and floor are covered in tiny mosaic tiles that are neutral in colour in daylight, but glow azure blue when it's dark – very impressive. During the day, you can get the same effect by cupping your hands over your eyes and leaning again a wall or pillar. This gives you the bright, almost fluorescent, blue glow from these little wonders.

"These little wonders" have been supplied by Yorkshire-based Prices Paving & Tile who can be found at the wonderfully-named village of Snape near Bedale, up in the North Yorkshire Moors. The fact that their office and showroom address is "The Stone Yard" will give you a clue. It's not unadjacent to nearby stone quarries.

But when you visit "The Stone Yard", be prepared for something unusual. This is nothing like the traditional sales area adjunct to a quarry, rough and ready with minimal facilities for customers. On the contrary, it's more of an experience than a showroom. You do in fact pass through a labyrinth of showrooms, each one leading to the next, and each one with its own particular theme. There's a complete contrast of atmospheres, from an Ancient Egyptian tomb - complete with stone sarcophagus! - to a slick Art Deco bathroom with its contemporary furniture. The idea is that people will be talking about the showroom as much as the products it displays. "The Stone Yard"

Stone floor - Opus pattern

Living room floor - Opus pattern

Bathroom wall - Coursed

Master bathroom

Jacuzzi, pool tiling

Pool column detail

Master suite

Pool steps

Mosaic tile colour contrast - shown in daylight and in the dark

is now a place to visit just to see it, even if you don't want to buy tiles (but you probably will!).

For all its Yorkshire roots, Prices Paving – a family firm run by Edward Price – sources its materials from far and wide. The stone used for the floors – and some of the walls – in Tindale Towers comes all the way from Israel. The 1,100 square metres of stone flooring rejoices in the name of "Brushed Jerusalem" and is laid in "Opus" pattern. The 400 square metres of stone on the walls is from the same material as the floors, but is coursed.

Stone floors have several advantages. Not only do they look good and require minimal maintenance, they are also very suitable for under-floor heating, which TT has throughout. The stone slabs are laid on the floor with a "marble fix" white adhesive, rather than the normal grey adhesive. With the grey type, the colour can rise up through the stone and discolour it from underneath.

The mosaic tiles around the pool are laid and sealed with a special sealant, grouted and then sealed again. There are hundreds of thousands of them. Just think about that, the next time you lay some tiles around your bath top!

Price's Paving Showroom

Stone storage yard - one of four

Leafy passage   Pictures by Joanne Garlick

Prices Paving & Tile Ltd
Natural Stone Importers
The Stone Yard
Snape
Bedale
North Yorkshire
Tel: 01677 470 999/470 599
Tel/fax: 01677 470 888
Email: sales@pricespaving.co.uk
Web: www.pricespaving.co.uk

Chapter Eighteen

A19 Pools & Spas

Making a splash

Mike Keen's very particular requirements for the basement swimming pool at Tindale Towers gave brothers Nigel and Glen Fallow of A19 Pools & Spas very particular headaches. For a start, the pool was kidney-shaped to Mike's design. Then he added a hot tub, again to his own design. Then there's the hot tub on the penthouse balcony, overlooking the Durham countryside.

"There are three types of pools," explains Nigel, "the traditional concrete tiled pool, the tank-lined pool and the all-in-one mono block. Mike chose the traditional design, which also happens to be the most expensive. Mike decided he wanted a level deck rather than a freeboard pool with the water level six or eight inches below the sides. That means installing an overflow grating all around the pool, with an underfloor balance tank.

"There are three electronic probes in the balance tank. One regulates the flow,

Tindale Towers Pool

Peter Davies

Building the pool

another activates the water feed if the water level gets too low, and the other sets off an alarm if the pool overflows and there is any risk of flooding. This is the most complicated job we have ever done."

The kidney-shaped pool measures about eight by four metres, and the spa or hot tub with its array of water jets is two metres in diameter. The pool is 1.2 metres (four feet) deep throughout. The water in the pool and the air in the pool room are heated separately, and dehumidifiers ensure the atmosphere is not too humid. There is plenty of room for people to sit around the pool, which also has a steam room and two toilets-cum-changing rooms.

Nigel and Glen are two of six brothers – they have no sisters – whose parents ran the family building firm, Wearside Contractors. Nigel qualified as a civil engineer and Glen as a mechanical engineer and both had successful careers overseas. Two brothers stayed with the family business, and the other two forged careers of their own outside the building trade.

Returning to the UK to settle down and bring up their families, Nigel and Glen set up A19 Pools & Spas in 1997. "We are now the biggest in our field in the north east," says Nigel proudly.

Peter Davies

A19 Pools & Spas
Pool House
White House Way
Peterlee
Co. Durham SR8 2RA
Tel: 0191 586 5002
Fax: 0191 586 5001
Email: haltduk@aol.com
Web: www.a19poolsandspas.co.uk

Chapter Nineteen

John Willetts

Versatile granite

It's perhaps no surprise that Mike Keen and his partner Julie Holliday chose granite for their worktops, window cills and lift doorway surrounds at Tindale Towers. And it's not because various famous footballers (and their WAGs) have done the same; rather it's for the same reasons as these high-profile, high-spending members of society. For a start, granite – a dense, igneous rock for the uninitiated - is a stunningly beautiful stone. It is extremely hard-wearing, obviously, but less obviously granite is also an extremely versatile natural material.

Granite is now used in all kinds of ways in the home: kitchen worktops and breakfast bars come immediately to mind, but granite is also used for window-cills and, remarkably, for free-standing furniture. Granite has been used for centuries to create handsome fireplaces. Remember all those old fireplaces we used to tear out in the sixties and seventies? Since the eighties, we've all been putting them back in again – and new, old-style ones too.

The granite for TT has been supplied and fitted by John Willetts, a local lad who has built up his business from scratch. John began putting in fireplaces as a hobby when he was working as a wagon-driver. He went full-time nearly forty years ago, and now has 32 employees and two depots. Willetts Fireplaces is still a family-run business, a close partnership of John and his wife Anne. The main Willetts showroom at Spennymoor, midway

Kitchen tops and work surfaces supplied by John Willetts of Spennymoor

Photographs by Peter Davies

- 66 -

John & Anne Willetts and staff (l-r): Anne, Julie, John, Val, Lucy

Lift surround

Window cill

Fireplaces on show

One of the John Willetts "Hole-in-the-Wall" Living Flame Effect Fires at Tindale Towers

(l-r): Willetts installers John Dodds, John Naylor, Barry Beadle

Spennymoor showrooms & offices

Pictures by Chris Foote Wood

between Bishop Auckland and Durham, is an Alladin's cave of fireplaces and much else, with realistic fires and comfortable armchairs to put you in the mood. Staff need to check at closing time to make sure no-one has fallen asleep in front of the fire! The other Willetts showroom is at Wrekenton near Gateshead.

John and his teams of installers work all over the North East of England. His clients include quite a number of those aforesaid premiership footballers (note: at the time of writing, there are three premiership soccer teams in the northeast) and their WAGs, plus other "well-known names" that John is sworn not to divulge. Suffice to say the Willetts lads have installed kitchen-tops and fireplaces at certain addresses in Darras Hall near Newcastle and at Wynyard Park near Stockton.

Willetts supplied Tindale Towers with its curved kitchen worktops, all the window-cills, and even the lift surrounds. There are two Willetts fires in TT, both lit by "Living Flames". The granite used is brown Amerello Gold from Brazil, which arrived in County Durham via a firm in Portugal who import it in bulk and cut it up into the 3cm (one and quarter inch) thick slabs needed.

"The world is getting smaller all the time," says John Willetts, "we source our materials from Italy, Portugal, Spain and even China."

John Willetts Fireplaces
Cambridge Street
Spennymoor
Co.Durham DL16 6DF
Tel: 01388 817 296
Fax: 01388 811 463
Email: jwilletts@hotmail.com
Web: www.johnwillettsfireplaces.co.uk

Chapter Twenty

Terence Hardy

Curvacious kitchen

A unique house needs a unique kitchen. To create that special kitchen, Mike Keen brought in the highly talented local artist and designer Terence Hardy who came up with a highly unusual and bespoke design. Like all the main rooms in Tindale Towers, the kitchen is spacious and has great views over the Durham countryside. With an enormous amount of space to fill, and to make best use of the layout, Terence created his bold and very curvaceous design. This matches the other rounded features of the house, such as the spiral staircase and the rounded corners on some of the walls.

Building curved units and doors presented major challenges to the manufacturing process, successfully overcome in Terence 's workshop and in the on-site fitting. The result has been the creation of a stunning but highly practical kitchen. It takes very special skills of design and manufacture to create curved kitchen units that not only look good but have doors and drawers that glide open and close with minimal effort.

Terence Hardy has always been interested in wood craft. From an early age he realised he could use his practical skills to create practical but good-looking furniture. Terry developed his interest and honed his skills by working with a number of well-established and highly-regarded furniture manufacturers, including Anthony Nixon and LJB Designs. Through this experience he developed a depth of

manufacturing and design capabilities and expertise on bespoke applications for wood.

In 2003 Terence set up Terence Hardy as a specialist business to design and manufacture bespoke items of furniture. His aim is to offer a highly personal service and give his clients the opportunity to express their own designs and ideas, and to combine these with Terry's own expertise, creativity and manufacturing skills to deliver a first class product.

Terry recently completed a commission to design and build a new kitchen in an 1870 Victorian vicarage (see page 70).

This was an unusual layout, and Terence had to combine modern equipment and clean lines with the historical and traditional feel of the period. He designed and built the wall units to be significantly taller than 'standard' kitchen size, to compensate for the high ceilings. This has created a balance of proportion, ideally suited to this handsome building. The owners had particular ideas and requirements of their own, which were successfully incorporated in the finished layout, and they were delighted with the result and the functionality of their kitchen space.

With these, and all of Terence Hardy's creations - which aren't restricted to kitchens - the client has an important say in every aspect of the work: from design ideas to layout and colours, and an opportunity to see each item in the workshops as it is being built and before it is delivered.

With his reputation and his business both growing fast, Terence Hardy has recently moved to new premises on the outskirts of Barnard Castle. His modern, well-equipped workshop and his skilled and increasing workforce provide the high level of back-up and support needed to supply the increasing demands of today's clients. Terence's relationship with his clients continues with a first-class after-sales and support service, an unusual level of investment in this field.

Pictures by Peter Davies

TERENCE HARDY

BESPOKE KITCHENS AND FURNITURE

Terence Hardy
Bespoke Kitchens and Furniture
2D Stainton Grove Industrial Estate
Barnard Castle
Co. Durham DL12 8UJ
Tel: 01833 630 002
Email: terry@terryhardy.co.uk
Web: www.terencehardy.co.uk

Chapter Twenty-one

Choice Linens

Elegance & style

"A Shildon lad and proud of it" is how Joe Walters describes himself. Shildon has been a railway town ever since 1825 when it was the venue for the first passengers to board the first train – Locomotion No. 1 – on its first historic journey on the world's first passenger railway, the Stockton & Darlington line which in fact started at Witton Park near Bishop Auckland. The line passed close by where Tindale Towers now stands.

Joe's dad, who died at 57, was a railway platelayer, very much in the Shildon tradition. Joe and his brother Anthony – seven years younger – broke with that tradition, finding their own way in life. Joe went into textiles and Anthony became a solicitor. After leaving Shildon All Saints School at 15, Joe was taken on as an apprentice overlooker at the John Binns weaving shed in Shildon. "Their main line was making the material for lining coffins," recalls Joe with a smile.

When John Binns was taken over by Vyella, they closed down the Shildon factory. At 21, Joe moved on to become an overlooker at Paton & Baldwin's Darlington factory. "It was all wool," recalls Joe, "basically, the sheepskins came in at one end and balls of wool went out the other." After a few years that factory also closed, and Joe "went on the road" as a travelling salesman, selling to shops and factories.

Sun Lounge: Charlotte Voile curtains mounted on electric track
Peter Davies

Joe did well and eventually became sales director, only to move on to selling car accessories with another company when he was enticed to leave the industry for a while. After moving to Nottingham, with a good salary and a company car, Joe yearned for two things – to get back to his native Durham and to start his own business. "I'd always wanted to run my own business, but I had to start small," he says.

"Small" meant a tiny shop unit in Darlington in 1985. With his wife Mary running party plans in the evenings to help the family finances, Joe hit on the idea of lunchtime factory sales selling bedding and accessories. They proved so popular that within a year Joe could afford the ideal premises for his ideal business – Choice Linens in Bishop Auckland's main shopping street, Newgate Street. He's been there ever since.

"It was always 'Choice.' In retail, you must always give the customers a choice," says Joe. When he first set up in Bishop, Joe was able to get a good supply of Marks & Spencer's "seconds." "They were like gold dust," says Joe, who became the main source of supply for miles around. Ten years ago, the M&S seconds dried up, and Joe added blinds, custom-made and ready-made curtains and cushions and a full range of bedding and linens.

Fitting out Tindale Towers from top to bottom has been the biggest single domestic order Joe has ever been asked to fulfil. "We supplied Mike Keen with a complete set of custom-made curtains and blinds," explains Joe, "Mike's brief was to make everything look rich but modern, and so we have used a modern velvet. There are no tie-backs or valances. So everything has clear lines, clean and elegant, nothing fussy." All the major windows – around forty - in Tindale Towers have electrical tracks. This proved a tricky job for the many curved windows in the house. The one fitted in the TT Sun Lounge is the biggest curved electric curtain track Broadstairs-based manufacturers Silent Gliss have ever made.

Going into Choice is like entering a Sultan's palace. Fabrics of every kind hang on every side in a profusion of colours and textures. Joe the salesman takes over. "We have a full range of household textiles and linens, tea-towels, sheets, pillows, towels, bedspreads, bedding, Roman blinds, wooden blinds, roller blinds, ready-made and custom-made curtains," he emphasises.

Equally enthusiastic are Joe's four permanent staff, Allyson Douthwaite, Lucy Allchurch, Joanne Davidson and Sandra (San) Beaumont. Allyson and Joanne have both been with Joe for over twenty years after joining as YTS trainees. Joe's wife Mary is still very much part of the business, looking after the administration. They have a son, Jos, who "has a good job in IT" according to his proud father.

"We pride ourselves on our product range – from a tea-towel to custom-made curtains - and our customer service. Our range is regularly updated with the latest styles, fashions and designs, whilst maintaining classics that never lose their appeal. There's something for everyone at choice. We believe we have the best selection of household textiles in the area – and we welcome commercial customers. We have a free home measuring and design service available and we offer a fitting service.

"I love my work," says Joe – this much is so obvious, he scarcely need say it.

Master Bedroom: Carnival Velvet curtains mounted on electric track
Peter Davies

At the counter: (l-r) Allyson Douthwaite, Lucy Allchurch, Joanne Davidson, Sandra Beaumont, Joe Walters of Choice

Joe Walters and the fabric shop he established in Newgate Street, Bishop Auckland

Joe and his staff, always ready to welcome customers

Chapter Twenty-two

Sarner-Tech

Lightweight flat-roof waterproofing

Do you suffer from interstitial condensation? (*). For flat roofs, it can be terminal. With a flat roof integral to Mike Keen's Art Deco house, Middlesbrough-based roofing specialists Sarner-Tech were brought in to provide Tindale Towers' flat, waterproof roof. While the Sarner-Tech system is utterly modern, the firm itself goes back nearly a century. Sarner-Tech boss Alan Ayres is the grandson of the founder and followed his father into the business. Sarner-Tech is now part of the R C Ayres company.

Charles Henry Ayres was clearly not a superstitious man. A slater and tiler by trade, he started up his roofing business on 13th March 1915. His son Ronald Cranston Ayres took over, followed by the present company director Alan Charles Ayres who joined the family firm when he left school at the age of fifteen.

The Sarner-Tech system is as simple as it is effective. First, a VCL (vapour-controlled layer) which is glued to the flat roof, which in this case made of concrete. A four-inch thick insulation layer comes next, and finally a single-ply pvc sheet is hot-air welded on to face the elements. This construction is known as a "warm roof" as it stops heat escaping.

Sarner-Tech quantity surveyor Damian Hunt sizes up each job, Alan Ayres does the estimating, contracts manager Ged Finnegan manages the project. Sarner-Tech also has a staff of thirty-six roofers who work in teams of two. The firm is "totally committed" to safety training, and has won several safety awards including those from Dupont and the National Federation of Roofing Contractors. On display in the boardroom is the silver tray, tea and coffee service awarded by the Federation to the late R C Ayres.

Sarner-Tech do all types of industrial and commercial roofing, traditional and modern, including slating, clay & concrete tiling, cedarwood shingles, built-up felt roofing, modern single-ply polymeric roof systems, and profiled metal sheeting. The company has been approved Sarnafil contractors since 1984, the same year it won a Civic Trust award for the refurbishment of the Old Town Hall at Middlesbrough. There was another Civic Trust award for the firm's work on the listed Ivy Cottage at Cowpen Bewley, reputedly the oldest dwelling-house in the old Cleveland area, helping restore it from complete dereliction.

Sarnafil is a high-performance roofing membrane which can either be fully adhered, as at Tindale Towers, or can be mechanically fastened. It comes in six standard colours and can also incorporate graphics which are hot-welded on. One spectacular example is the Olympic Oval in Salt Lake City for the 2002 Winter Olympics - although Sarner-Tech didn't do that particular job.

Sarner-Tech has an impressive list of clients who include British Telecom, ICI, Ladbrokes, North and South Tees Health Authorities, the Universities of Teesside, Durham & Northumbria, the North-Eastern Co-op, the Sears Group, Zeneca and many more. The firm offers a 24-hour service for maintenance and repairs.

(*) Interstitial condensation – that's when the layers in a flat roof begin to part; water gets in the gap; the dew point is reached; you get interstitial condensation; your roof starts to fail.

The Coleridge Centre adjoins Skerne Park Primary School

Chris Foote Wood

Sarner-Tech guys making sure the flat roof at Skerne Park School in Darlington is made absolutely water-tight. (l-r): Tony Lane (Foreman), Graham Loughborough, Adam Aylott.

Chris Foote Wood

Chapter Twenty-three

Sykes Specialist Contracting

Making the White House white

When you see Tindale Towers for the first time, several things strike you at once. First, its unusual design. There aren't many Art Deco buildings in County Durham, let alone in Bishop Auckland. Then there's the size – it's quite big for a house, isn't it? Then there's the colour – slightly off-white in fact, but dazzling white in the sun (we hope!). That white rendering, pure and smooth, was put on by Sykes Specialist Contracting Ltd using the patent Alumasc Silicone Render System.

A good finish

PlanArch Design

Alumasc is not your usual rendering system. Chris Sykes the company owner explains: "Traditional rendering systems have to be mixed on site and that gives you a problem of consistency. They are also heavy and difficult to apply. Alumasc is a lightweight, proprietory rendering system which can be applied to all types of masonry substrate. The system is applied with a base coat which is fully reinforced with a glassfibre reinforcing mesh. This is subsequently primed and then finished with a self-coloured silicone compound render available in over 400 colours. Not only is there absolute quality control, a perfect finish is guaranteed. As Sykes are Alumasc's leading North East approved installer, all Sykes operatives have been trained by Alumasc, and pride themselves in achieving a quality finish and above all find the Alumasc render products to be one of if not the best in the UK."

As well as the outside of Tindale Towers, Chris – or rather his merry men – have plastered all the inside walls to give them an as near perfect, lasting finish as possible. Extensive curved walls including a four storey spiral stair case provided Chris's men with a challenge which was successfully met by his team. For "merry men" read "merry men and a woman" because Chris has recruited what is, in these days of equality, still a rarity – a female plasterer. Kimberley Segger is the real deal. Recently CITB (Construction Industry Training Board) qualified, Kimberley is set on making a career in applying specialist render finishes, and can quite easily hold her own in what was and still is a male-dominated industry.

Company owner Chris Sykes was born and brought up in Blackpool, but settled in the North East after taking a degree in building & design at Newcastle University. Chris has a background in construction – his parents still run their long-established family building business which was established by Chris's grandfather after the end of the first world war. Grandfather Arthur was a plumber by trade and went on to build houses, as well as running his plumbing company. Chris's father Alan continued with the family business, building houses and moving the company forward - even taking on a contract in Ibiza! Chris however decided to do his own thing and went to work for Tarmac Construction as senior surveyor, working on the building of RNAD Coulport, a Nuclear Submarine Base. Chris also has a sister who has a completely different profession. Currently she is accident and emergency registrar at a hospital in Leeds. Chris's father says: "It's great to see my children have the strength of character and determination to be successful in stressful and demanding professions."

On his return to the UK, Chris then had fifteen years with Alumasc before deciding to go back into mainstream contracting in 2006, and he now runs his own business as a specialist contractor. As business manager for Alumasc, Chris reported direct to the managing director Mr Robert Littlewood. Based in Newcastle but covering the whole of the UK, Chris was responsible for all of Alumasc's Facades operations. Running his own company is "hectic, challenging and enjoyable," says Chris. Robert Littlewood says: "Chris is very passionate about his

Smooth surface

PlanArch Design

The finished job

PlanArch Design

business, and together with his excellent technical knowledge and ability to role up his sleeves when required, makes a solid foundation for a good job done: a great guy to work with and for."

Offering "21st century insulated facades", Chris says: "Sykes Specialist Contracting Ltd is a leading northern installer of external wall insulation and lightweight render finishes, with over 15 years' experience in the use of EWI (external wall insulation) systems and renders in both social housing refurbishment and new build applications. Sykes Specialist Contracting Ltd provide a fully integrated package through expertise and quality of installation, offering best value to its clients. We have an extensive knowledge in material and system selection offering impartial advice, combined with technical expertise, advising on detailing, budget costs and programme."

Chris Sykes
Sykes Specialist Contracting Ltd
(render system by Alumasc)
Unit A11
Design Works
William Street
Felling NE10 0JP
Tel: 0191 423 6200
Fax: 0191 423 6201
Email: info@sykessc.co.uk
Web: www.sykessc.com

Chapter Twenty-four

Camedia

Discreet security

With such a large and prominent building as Tindale Towers, security has to be a prime consideration – but TT is a house and a home, and the security has to be discreet. It is. The only exception is a pair of "swan neck" towers, prominent at opposite corners of the site. They couldn't be anything else but prominent, as they give an overview of the exterior of the house, the garden, access roads and parking areas. They can pan, tilt and zoom to home in on any intruder, human, animal or bird.

But, very discreet and almost hidden away, are a number of tiny, almost invisible security cameras at various points inside and outside the building. The images from these cameras – there are at least twenty of them - can all be monitored from the control centre inside the house, which has a multiple-image television screen and controls to delight any security officer. One mundane task is to view visitors to TT. When you call at the main gate, you buzz, someone answers – this can be done from

Tindale Towers owner Mike Keen at the controls of his security centre in the house. At the time this picture was taken, Mike (who makes furniture) hadn't got around to providing himself with a chair!

The two "swan neck" towers which can show every part of the outside of Tindale Towers and its grounds

Mike Keen opens the entrance gates to TT via a key pad. There's one on every floor.

Pictures by Chris Foote Wood

any phone in the house – and "open sesame" the main gate glides to one side to admit you, if you are recognised, that is. There are keypads on every floor to operate the gates. On driving away, the exit gate opens automatically as you approach.

All this up-to-date, high-tec equipment, CCTV, intruder and fire alarms, has been supplied and installed by Camedia Security Ltd. Camedia has been established for seven years. Its headquarters are in Richmond, North Yorkshire, and it has a base at Newton Aycliffe, seven miles from Tindale Towers. The company operates emergency response and has 24-hour call-out and monitoring.

"We specialise in the installation and maintenance of electronic security systems, CCTV, intruder alarms, access control, fire, digital recording and remote monitoring," says Camedia managing director Lee Davies, "All our systems and procedures are of the highest quality. We are ISO9001 compliant and NSI (*) gold approved installers. It is well established that surveillance cameras can reduce theft by 50 per cent. We offer a complete design, build and installation service for residential, office and commercial premises. That's what we do, we do it to the highest standards, and we're proud of having many glowing references from satisfied customers."

(*) National Security Inspectorate

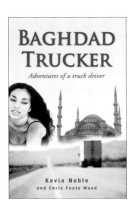

BAGHDAD TRUCKER
(Northern Writers 2006)
The true-life adventures of a long-distance truck driver who helped pioneer the overland route to the Middle East on "the most dangerous roads in the world." As co-author, with Kevin Noble.

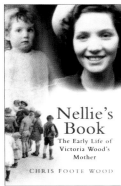

NELLIE'S BOOK – THE EARLY LIFE OF VICTORIA WOOD'S MOTHER
(Sutton Publishing 2006)
FOREWORD BY VICTORIA WOOD. Surviving poverty in industrial Manchester in the 1920s and 1930s. Helen Colleen (Nellie) Mape, born 1919, was one of eight children born to very poor Irish Catholic parents. Nellie worked full-time at a steelworks from the age of fourteen, met her husband Stanley Wood at eighteen, and by the end of WW2 was married with two children. "Nellie's Book" is the remarkably detailed story of a girl growing up in real poverty, telling how her large working-class family managed to stay above the breadline. Based on her notes and essays – in later life Nellie gained a BA degree and an MA. She died in 2001, with her writings largely unpublished. This is her story, much in Nellie's own words.

KINGS OF AMATEUR SOCCER
(North Press 1985)
The official centenary history of Bishop Auckland Football Club, ten times FA Amateur Cup winners and the most famous and successful amateur soccer club of all time.

BISHOP AUCKLAND IN OLD PICTURE POSTCARDS
(European Library 1985)
Local history in words and pictures.

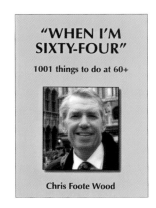

WHEN I'M SIXTY-FOUR –
1001 things to do at 60+
(Capall Bann 2007)
Inspirational lifestyle advice for the ever-increasing numbers of active older people.

LIFE OF BRIAN IN BLACK & WHITE –
Fifty years following Newcastle United
by Brian Hall
(Northern Writers, December 2007)
With cartoons by Paul Burke. Amusing, very personal story of a dedicated Newcastle United fan, the highs and lows of Brian's life mirroring the ever-changing fortunes of the club. "By a fan for the fans." Edited by Chris Foote Wood.

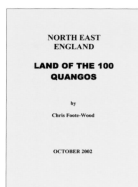

LAND OF THE 100 QUANGOS
(North Press 2002)
An expose of the 100-plus appointed and largely unknown government-funded organisations who run the North East.

PUBLISHING SEPTEMBER 2008:
Local Hero – the Glenn McCrory Story
[working title – may be changed]
Chris Foote-Wood has ghost-written this authorized autobiography of Glenn McCrory, the only boxer from the North East ever to win a world title.

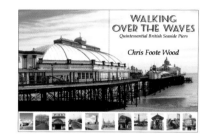

WALKING OVER THE WAVES –
Quintessential British Seaside Piers
(Whittles Publishing, March 2008)
In 2007, author Chris Foote Wood visited every one of the 50+ piers still in existence around the coasts of England and Wales. This is the story of his fascinating odyssey in words and pictures. Packed with information, statistics and scintillating stories. Lavishly illustrated with over 250 old and new photographs.

PROUD TO BE A GEORDIE –
the life & legacy of Jack Fawcett
(Dysart Associates 2007)
Authorised biography of Jack Fawcett, the miner's son who developed the Newcastle Business Park and other major projects in the North East and elsewhere. Private publication – not for sale. Can be viewed.

Most of Chris's books are available from major booksellers, or on-line from Ebay, Amazon and Chris's website www.writersinc.biz. To get your story published, visit www.writersinc.biz. For details of the wide range of work Chris does, visit www.northernwriters.co.uk. Chris is happy to give "Author Talks" to local groups and organizations. Contact him at "Wor Hoos" 28 Cockton Hill Road, Bishop Auckland, Co. Durham DL14 6AH.
Tel: 01388 605181; Fax: 01388 450450; Email: footewood@btconnect.com

Thanks

So many people have helped me produce this book, I cannot list them all. Suffice to say, I am grateful to each and every one of the twenty-plus companies and individuals who have contributed to this unique publication (see list of sponsors). In particular, Colling Morris of PlanArch Design has had a major input "over and above the call of duty." Peter Davies has taken many of the superb photographs essential to this book. Printers Lintons of Crook have again done a first-class job, turning my rough layout sketches into the real thing.

Most of all I must of course thank Tindale Towers owner Mike Keen who has been more than generous in supporting this venture. Thanks too go to Peter in the Keenpine office, always ready with a reviving cup of coffee. Special thanks go to Mike's partner Julie, who has let me have the run of the house, and to his children, James, Adam and Emma who have allowed us to photograph their bedrooms(!). And to my dear wife Frances for her love and understanding.

Chris Foote Wood
Author, Editor & Publisher
Bishop Auckland, January 2008

Sponsors

A19 POOLS & SPAS Swimming Pools & Spas (Chapter 18)
ANTHONY WALTERS Solicitors (Ch 7)
ARRAN CONSTRUCTION Main contractors (Ch 8)
BDN LTD Structural design (Ch 5)
CAMEDIA SECURITY LTD Security systems (Ch 24)
CHOICE LINENS Curtains (Ch 21)
EVERSHED PRODUCTS Balcony decking & gate panels (Ch 15)
GILWOOD ENGINEERING Heating system, air exchange, rainwater recycling (Ch 12)
HAZELHURST CCS Quantity Surveyors (Ch 6)
JMW ALUMINIUM External windows & doors (Ch 14)
KEENPINE Furniture (Ch 27)
LEEMING ASSOCIATES Landscape Architects (Ch 25)
MILLENIUM DECORATORS (Ch 26)
NORTH YORKSHIRE TIMBER Doors & wood surrounds (Ch 16)
PLANARCH DESIGN Architects & planners (Ch 4)
PRICES PAVING & TILES Floor & wall tiles (Ch 17)
PRIORY SAFETY SERVICES Health & Safety (Ch 9)
ROGER BULLIVANT Piling (Ch 10)
SARNER-TECH Roofing contractors (Ch 22)
SYKES SPECIALIST CONTRACTORS Render systems (Ch 23)
TERENCE HARDY BESPOKE Custom-built kitchens (Ch 20)
TOMLINSON-LONGSTAFF Electrical Engineers (Ch 11)
WILLETTS FIREPLACES Worktops & fireplaces (Ch 19)
ZENEX Heating systems (Ch 13)

References & further reading:

Art Deco Architecture in New York, 1920-1940, Don Vlack, Harper & Row 1974. ISBN 0064388506.

Skyscraper Style: Art Deco New York, Cervin Robinson & Rosemarie Haag Bletter, Oxford University Press, 1975. ISBN 0195018737.

The Art Deco skyscraper in New York, Norbert Messler, P Lang 1986. ISBN 0820401587.

American Art Deco, Alastair Duncan, Abrams1986. ISBN 0810918501.

Art Deco Architecture, Patricia Bayer, Thames & Hudson 1992. ISBN 0500341222.

Deco by the Bay: Art Deco architecture in the San Francisco Bay area, Michael F Crowe, Penguin 1995. ISBN 0525938567 (cased); 0525486216 (pbk).

A journey through American Art Deco: architecture, design, and cinema in the twenties and thirties, Giovanna Franci, University of Washington Press 1997. ISBN 0295976535.

A Spirit of Progress: Art Deco Architecture in Australia, Patrick van Daele & Roy Lumby, G+B Arts International, 1997. ISBN 9057036711.

Art Deco of the Palm Beaches, Ingrid Cranfield, David & Charles 2001. ISBN 0715309641 (cased) 071531744X (pbk).

The Art Deco house: avant-garde houses of the 1920s and 1930s, Adrian Tinniswood., Mitchell Beazley 2002. ISBN 1840003952 (cased) 184533180X (pbk).

American Art Deco Architecture, Carla Breeze, WW Norton 2003. ISBN 0393019705.

Houses of the Art Deco years, Jean Gardner, Braiswick 2003. ISBN 1898030715.

Art Deco London, Colin Michael Hines & Keith Chetham, 2003.

Art Deco New York, David Garrard Lowe, Watson-Guptill Publications, 2004. ISBN 0823002845.

Art Deco House Style: An Architectural and Interior Design Source Book, Ingrid Cranfield, 2004.

London Art Deco: A Celebration of the Architectural Style of the Metropolis during the Twenties & Thirties, Arnold Schwartzman, 2007.

Bombay Art Deco Architecture: A Visual Journey: 1930-1953, Navin Ramani & Laura Cerwinske, 2007.

Art Deco of the Palm Beaches - Images of America, Sharon Koskoff, Arcadia Publishing, 2007.

Websites:

www.london-footprints.co.uk/artdecobldgs.htm
www.achome.co.uk/artdeco
www.worldcollectorsnet.com/artdeco
www.thehistorychannel.co.uk/site/encyclopedia/article_show/art_deco
www.artlex.com/ArtLex/a/artdeco.html
www.wikipedia.org